I was shivering and sweating, my nose pouring that liquid snot that always signifies the beginning of something awful. Stupidly, I had put the wet, freshly clipped pot into a plastic, grocery store bag and threw it into the car. The pot was starting to mold and there was nowhere to dry it in the shack we were using so I thought I'd bring it home. Only minutes from the shack, the little car chugged down a steep hill into a police roadblock. I couldn't believe that I had been stupid enough or unlucky enough to be arrested a second time.

Published by
Zumaya Publications
P.O. Box 44062
Burnaby, B.C. V5B 4Y2
Canada

ISBN 1-894869-54-0

Kim,
Everything you always wanted to know about my life ... with a grain of salt.

EVERYTHING'S GOING TO POT

BY

MARY-JANE BRYDE

Love
Deirdre

Dedication:

I had always intended to dedicate this book to the two most important men in my life- my incredible husband and my father, Peter. On May 18, 2002, that changed when we lost a dear friend and the world lost an amazing young man.

This book is dedicated to the memory of Jamie Ross; brother, grower, father, friend.

"Whom the Gods love dies young." Menander, 342-292 B.C.

PREFACE

Everyone sees the truth through his or her own eyes; and, often, our vision is clouded. This story is my vision, my truth the way I saw things as they happened around me. Some conversations and events that I was not present for have had to be reconstructed. This was done by interviewing all involved parties and presenting facts and words, where possible, along with filling in the blanks with what I felt would best embody the truth.

> *"Truth itself does not have the privilege to be employed at any time and in every way. Its use, noble as it is, has its circumscriptions and limits."*
> *Montaigne (1533-1592)*

Marijuana has been the subject of myth and controversy for centuries; but to me, marijuana is, quite simply, a plant. Period. Like any other plant on earth, it has specific growing requirements, a unique scent and a characteristic vegetative and flowering cycle.

People create opinions and myths and pass them along to others. And people have vastly differing opinions about this particular herb. Some believe it to be a gateway drug— the very thing that could lead you down the road to ruin—yet others believe it to be a medicinal, healing herb, the very thing to open doors to a spiritual world or alleviate pain and suffering.

Some of the many myths surrounding marijuana are that it's fun, easy and lucrative to grow. And like other myths about marijuana— that it will make you crazy, that it leads to heroin addiction or causes fetal abnormalities when smoked by pregnant mothers—they simply aren't true.

Because of this controversial history, strong opinions continue to be formed based on decades of ignorance and misinformation. This is especially true of those who have never grown or used the herb.

For some, the plant grows well, lining their pockets with undeclared cash; but others are plagued by disease and disaster and never experience any degree of success. Millions of people love and worship this plant, working the use of its dried flowers and leaves into part of their daily routine. Many use marijuana for its proven medicinal properties, such as alleviating the pain and nausea associated with cancer, glaucoma, AIDS and chemotherapy. And some people are neutral, like the vegetarian who doesn't object to eating meat but just simply chooses not to.

That was how I'd always felt about marijuana—neutral. I didn't smoke it or grow it, but I certainly didn't find it offensive. All that changed when I fell in love with a man who grew marijuana. Now, I know a lot about this plant that is so loved and hated and feared and revered. I even consider myself somewhat of an expert on marijuana, and I want to share my story with any who care to read it. It's the story of my ten years as a full-time professional pot grower. It's also the story of my life, in a way, the first twenty-five years of which were not nearly as exciting as the last ten.

My introduction to the marijuana business coincided with my introduction to my husband. So, in a way, this is his story, too. Although it may seem unbelievable at times, everything you're about to read is true.

PROLOGUE

SEPTEMBER 9, 2000—I was shivering and sweating, my nose pouring that liquid snot that always signifies the beginning of something awful. Stupidly, I had put the wet, freshly clipped pot into a plastic grocery bag and thrown it into the car. The pot was starting to mold, and there was nowhere to dry it in the shack we were using; so I thought I'd take it home. Neither Mikayla, who was driving, nor I was worried about it a bit—I was so sick I didn't care about anything but getting home for a hot bath, Mikayla wasn't a paranoid person and felt safe in the sparsely populated wilderness community.

Only minutes from the shack, the little car chugged down a steep hill into a police roadblock.

Mikayla shrieked, "Oh, shit! It's a roadblock! What do I do? What should I do? Oh, my God! It's the police!"

I sat beside her, stunned—speechless, for once. I didn't really want to believe it was a roadblock. It was all happening too fast; but the car, the police cruisers with their lights flashing, Mikayla's mouth, everything seemed to be unfolding before me in slow motion. I had no idea what we should do, so I waited for the universe to take charge. I sat quietly and did nothing.

Shaking, Mikayla backed the car up to a side street that cut away from the main road, ground the transmission into second and slowly drove towards the end of a dead-end street. This made the police at the bottom of the hill immediately suspicious; and before we could unroll the window and throw the bag of pot out into the black, starless night we were surrounded.

There were two cops; one approached each door, and both started yelling questions at us. They informed us that the car reeked of marijuana, which was not exactly a newsflash to us. Within

1

seconds, we were both under arrest, although they hadn't yet found the bag of pot under my seat.

So, we were arrested for smelling like marijuana and backing away from a road check.

"It's mine." I admitted as I supplied the officer with my full name and address. "The pot is mine. Leave her alone." I told them Mikayla knew nothing about the plastic bag crammed under my seat, and that I alone should be arrested. But Mikayla had panicked; she was shaking, crying uncontrollably and buying into all the lies the policemen were telling her. She was talking.

After giving her the right to remain silent, the cop with the fat, girl-like ass started asking his quivering, blubbering prisoner a barrage of questions.

"Where did you just come from? Where did you obtain the marijuana? How long have you known her? Where's the grow house? Did you just come from a grow house? (The sheer ignorance of this question always floored me. A cop in a community literally saturated with thousands of pounds of outdoor-grown pot looking for a grow room. It was September, peak pot-harvest time; and yet he wanted Mikayla to show him a grow house that didn't exist.) Did you meet her husband? Were you in their house? To your knowledge, were there any drugs in the house? Did you see any drugs in the house? Is it full of expensive things; was the furniture nice? Did you know they're drug kingpins out here?" Blah, blah, blah.

Mikayla and I were separated.

Having the worst night of her life, trying to hold herself together and determined not to get me in any more trouble than I was already, Mikayla lead Constable Stark up and down several dirt roads that went nowhere. She honestly didn't know where she'd just come from; she had never been there before tonight. It was dark, there were almost no houses on a seven-kilometer stretch of road and if she saw a driveway that remotely looked like the one where we'd just been she pretended it was definitely the wrong place.

This went on for almost two hours, the cop finally giving up and driving back to the police station with his exhausted prisoner. Mikayla wouldn't know until weeks later, when we hired a lawyer to defend us, that she had been under no obligation to answer any of the questions she was asked. When she had been read her rights that fateful night, after every sentence, the constable paused and asked, "Do you understand this right?" Every time without exception, she had yelled, "No! I don't understand *anything* that's happening" through trembling lips erupting with saliva. Mikayla had been so intimidated that she felt she was under obligation to answer all of the questions the policeman asked her.

I sat and froze in the back of my own police cruiser while Constable Fat-Ass arranged for the impounding of Mikayla's car. I refused to speak, other than to ask for the heat to be turned on and to inform the young cop in charge of me of the absurdity of our drug laws. I watched out the window as he photographed evidence placed on the hood of the car: Mikayla's vitamins, my lunch box, my lunch, the wet pot, our scissors and various shots of the car. Soon, a tow truck arrived and hauled the little car to an impound lot. I watched the other police car, with my dear friend in the back, turn and go up the hill to where we had just come from. I prayed that Mikayla would hold herself together and not lead them to our property.

Maybe it was because I was sick that I didn't fully appreciate what had just happened. Or maybe I was having a hard time swallowing the fact that growing a forbidden plant in the wilderness could, in fact, lead to incarceration. Maybe because deep in the pit of my soul I felt that I deserved to be punished, I was calmly accepting my fate. I had been arrested for possession of marijuana and had admitted it was mine. The amount in the bag was large enough to get me a trafficking charge and probably also a charge for cultivation. Alone and helpless, I faced the possibility of a criminal record.

YEAR ONE, 1992

MICHAEL

JULY 10—*I woke up depressed and feeling like a failure. The humid little bedroom with pale-green walls and worn hardwood floors was causing me to feel claustrophobic. I have tried so hard to make my two-year marriage work; but as I looked over at the large snoring lump that is my husband, I wanted to cry, give up, admit defeat.*

It was the summer of 1992, and I was unhappily married and living in Vancouver. I desperately wanted to leave my husband and start fresh but couldn't find the courage to do so. Craig was a fun-loving man who happened to be unmotivated, slightly overweight and scarred from years of playing hockey and squashing pimples. He did nothing more expertly than smoke pot—every day, all day long—complemented by regular bouts of drinking, carousing and snorting cocaine. The previous night had been no exception, and my sensitive Irish nose had taken about all it could handle.

We struggled financially as most young couples do; but we always seemed to have enough money to keep Craig smoking, snorting and chugging. For as long as I could remember, I felt strongly that marriage was something I needed; and, for some reason, I'd promised myself to do it by age twenty-five. Craig was in the right place at the right time, and we exchanged New Age wedding vows on the back of a houseboat. The rest, as they say, is history.

Remembering my early beginnings and how helpful and wonderful Craig had been made me feel sad and guilty—the very emotions that were keeping me tied to the sinking ship. I'd come to the bustling West Coast city when I was in my early twenties, fresh out of nursing school, hoping to find a decent job and a safe place to live. For a small town girl, the city was overwhelming and intimidating. I met Craig, an outgoing lifetime resident; and he was like a gift from God.

Craig had been drafted to play pro hockey at seventeen but quit prematurely to look after his father, who battled lung cancer for seven years. Always involved in sports, music and social events, knowing every shortcut and good restaurant in the city, Craig soon opened my eyes to everything Vancouver had to offer; and I started to enjoy my new life in the city. We also became inseparable. I landed a live-in position in a group home for respirator-dependent quadriplegics, while Craig continued to work part-time for a lighting company.

My job paid well and was quite rewarding but eventually began to take its toll on me. With nothing functioning from the neck down, my patients were all very skilled at head games. By the end of two years I was physically and mentally exhausted. I no longer had any desire to wash another spastic penis or hold a burning cigarette to the lips of an eager quadriplegic. My back and wrists were weakened from the constant heavy lifting, and the politics and customs of nursing disgusted me.

I left the group home and became a private nurse for my favorite patient, Doug Vandermeer. He had managed to move out on his own after ten years in medical captivity. Doug didn't smoke cigarettes or drink booze until his wheelchair became a fermenting mixture of pee and wet sheepskin. This had been a favorite trick of most of the patients I cared for—healthy, vital young men who'd suddenly found themselves trapped inside a body that would no longer listen. Drugs and alcohol provided an easy escape for most, but Doug was different. He was rarely manipulative or demanding and quietly accepted his fate to remain in a wheelchair forever. He rented an apartment, and I began my new job as my marriage steadily disintegrated.

* * *

> JULY 11—*I woke up alone at five a.m. to a sky of such clarity and perfection that I knew today would be the day. I can't take another moment of being in limbo, not really living but playing a part in this marriage that is nothing but a lie. I want to be happy and passionate; I want to be single. With my stomach in knots and a full pot of coffee percolating, I waited for Craig's inevitable sneak through the front door. My hands trembled; I had to squeeze them around the steaming mug, burning myself to keep from splattering coffee all over. At eight-thirty, the door opened. After two years of unholy matrimony, I told my gray-faced, unsuspecting husband that I could no longer live with him. Without speaking a word, he walked to the spare bedroom, sat down at his desk and rolled a joint. He cried quietly but graciously accepted my decision and made plans to move out.*

I never had so much as a moment of regret or pity. The only thing I felt bad about was that I never missed the person I had shared my life with for the last five years. Our marriage had been doomed from day one because of me—I had never loved Craig as I should have.

My decision to get divorced lifted my spirits to a warm, lofty place filled with hope and lust. After one full week of being separated and single, I was invited to a huge country music (which I hate) festival in a tiny town in the mountains a few hours east of Vancouver. The plan was to camp with my newly married best friend from back home and have a girl's weekend.

* * *

JULY 19—*The site is beautiful. It looks like something out of an old western movie. We arrived early to get a good spot and spent the first day drinking, reminiscing and setting up our tent. Our home for the weekend was a tiny cheap assembly of nylon and plastic anchored to the ground with the equivalent of four toothpicks. The surrounding area is sand and sagebrush; none of the campsites have shade. It took less than an hour to make camp in the soft dusty field; and laughter, drinking and sunbathing filled the rest of our day. By evening, we were slightly sunburned and primed for going out.*

The most important feature of a large country music event is, of course, the beer gardens. I enjoyed this about as much as I enjoyed the music; but, since we were in the middle of nowhere, my options were pretty limited. I'd just spent most of the day sitting beside a flimsy tent, already filled with dust and mosquitoes, listening to blaring, distorted country tunes, many of which I was horrified to realize I recognized. In the beer gardens, my friend and I entertained ourselves by people-watching; and, after a few hours, I noticed a bright spot in the beer-swilling congregation. He was young, firm and gorgeous and had no visible tattoos or pockmarks.

I strategically threw myself in front of him, making sure my skimpy top was unbuttoned one more button; and I smoothed down my dust-filled mane of reddish-blonde hair. He smiled—a dazzling smile framed by long, wavy brown hair and huge blue eyes. His name was Bud. How appropriate for such an event.

Bud and I spent the rest of the evening together; and I lured him into our tent, where he spent the night—platonically. As morning came, with all three of us wedged together like sweaty sardines, Bud and I lay awake making plans for the day. By dinnertime we were no longer platonic.

I had probably had sex twice in the last six months, both times purely out of guilt and pity. The more drugs Craig had ingested, the more repulsive he'd become; and, during the final months of our marriage, I could barely stand to touch him. After that, offering myself to Bud was easy.

After some much-needed, pretty decent sex in a field overlooking the camping area, we had the requisite serious after-sex conversation. This included the "Did anyone ever really break your heart?" discussion. Bud had been stalked and tormented by his most recent girlfriend, who was also the daughter of his boss. She had the power to make life very difficult for him, but he had broken her heart by cheating on her. My only heartbreaker, I told him, had been an older guy who owned a nightclub and had an appetite for women and drugs. I honestly felt he might be dead of AIDS or a drug overdose or something equally sinister. Anyway, I told Bud, it had been years since I'd even heard Michael's name.

With that said, we headed out for another evening of country fun. With my best friend in tow, Bud and I lined up for drinks. I'd just settled into place in the long, undulating column filled with moustaches and cowboy boots when I felt someone staring at me. My friend poked me and whispered, "Isn't that Michael Hokenson?" And there he was, my real future husband—a tall, perfectly built blond with devilish green eyes and flawless skin.

This was the older guy who'd broken my heart when I was nineteen and just starting college for the first time. He'd been so intense and crazy I hadn't known how to handle him. He swept me off my feet and made me feel insecure, all at the same time. We had parted awkwardly, both being too full of pride to be honest about our feelings for each other. And now, years later, fate stepped in; and our worlds collided again.

He was standing in front of me, sporting a T-shirt that read "You Have Two Choices with Country Music...Love It or F**K Right Off." The mere sight of him mad my knees go week, and my heart pounded wildly in my chest.

Michael looked much healthier and fitter than I remembered. He was tanned and muscular, with clear eyes and had his long curly hair pulled back in a ponytail. We embraced tightly, and I marveled aloud at his transformation. This, he told me, was due to the fact he'd quit the liquor business and all the late-night parties that went with it two years earlier. He'd bought eighty acres of land and a rustic old cabin in the country and was making his living selling T-shirts at festivals and concerts. The T-shirt story was credible on the surface; but, let's face it—even a non-pot-smoking nurse from the city knows the only reason guys like Michael buy acreages in the country is to grow pot. So, I asked my future husband straight out if he had become a pot grower, and he assured me he had not. It was a lie, of course. Michael has a habit of lying, and he's really good at it.

It didn't really matter what Michael was growing in the bush. We were overwhelmingly attracted to each other; and he told me right then and there, in front of Bud and the entire bunch of sweaty, drunken country music fans, that he was going to marry me. All the feelings we'd had for each other years before came rushing back instantly. Not exactly lucky in love, I tried to fight what I was feeling and think with my head. Marriage was the last thing on my newly freed mind, and I was still technically married to Scar Face. Michael would have to do more to convince me of his metamorphosis.

Michael and I dated from that moment on—awkwardly, at first, with me somewhat suspicious and deliberating. I continued working live-in shifts as a private nurse for Doug while Michael remained in the bush two hundred-fifty miles away. I planned on moving slowly and not making any foolish decisions, but it was hard. Every time he kissed me and called me "Princess" or stroked my hair and smiled as I told him about work, I fell deeper and harder for the avenger in the forest.

* * *

SEPTEMBER 5—*He was waiting for me outside, sitting in the back of an old pickup, his legs dangling off the tailgate. He was grinning broadly, and I could see that he had something for me partly hidden behind his back.*

I had made the drive in five hours and forty-five minutes, a personal best. It was sunny and hot, and I had been living for these four days off with

Michael. With the sunroof and windows open, I filled my lungs with the warm, clean air, inhaling traces of pine, fir and sweet grasses. Rounding the last corner to the driveway, marked only with an overturned five-gallon bucket, I felt as if my heart would burst. I have missed Michael so intensely that I can hardly contain myself. I am beginning to feel more at home here, in the wilderness, than I do in the city surrounded by people and buildings and noise. I know I am in way over my head and completely in love with a crazy man living in a bus. I know that I am well on my way to a foolish decision.

That first fall we spent together was magical. I went to Michael's acreage for most of my days off, and we camped behind the dilapidated cabin in his ridiculously crooked and messy '55 Greyhound bus. There was a long, hot Indian summer that year, with fall temperatures hardly much different than summer. We spent our days hiking or swimming and our nights playing cards or just snuggling and talking in the candlelit bus.

Michael had been a notorious packrat all his life; and he had three old outbuildings and the main cabin full of boxes of junk, stacks of old magazines and books and an endless supply of weird things he'd collected. This provided him with materials for the freaky collages, booklets and letters I was now bombarded with, each gift full of relevant humor and incredible creativity. Never had anyone spent hours meticulously making me a card or gift in a world where everything is simply bought. For a man who'd had little nurturing from his eternally busy parents—an abusive, alcoholic father and globetrotting socialite mother—Michael was amazingly thoughtful and caring.

Other than selling T-shirts, Michael hadn't worked in almost a year following a serious car accident. He'd fallen asleep at the wheel of his SUV; and the cruise control stuck at seventy miles an hour, the vehicle uncontrollably rolling through ditches and across farmland with Michael trapped inside. Being highly disorganized, he had no insurance, just a B.C. permit that became invalid as soon as he crossed the Alberta border. He also had no medical coverage and didn't receive proper treatment for the serious injuries he suffered in the crash, including swelling of the brain, broken ribs, a broken wrist and bruising from head to toe.

The only thing that made the pain and loss tolerable was that he had fallen in love with and bought his land two years before his accident. With the bus to live in and no rent or mortgage to pay, he could rest and nurse himself back to health on his magical piece of wilderness. He was exhausted after years in the liquor business; fresh air, sunshine, beautiful vegetation and acres of silent privacy were just what his aching body needed. He was also embarrassed about the memory loss he'd developed from the accident and had no desire to be around people.

* * *

OCTOBER 17—*It was a radiant sunny afternoon, and the world looked magnificent all around us. The trees were vibrantly cloaked in oranges and yellows that only late October can boast. The last of the dragonflies had succumbed to fall, and the air was calm and quiet. Michael and I were lazing around in the bus after a late night when he jumped up and announced, "Put your hiking boots on, Princess. I want to show you something."*

I quickly got ready, and we wandered far away from the bus to the west side of the property. We climbed, hand in hand, up a steep hill dotted with Oregon grapes, bracken ferns, soapberries and young birch trees that had turned color. We stopped when we reached a small clearing framed by evergreens. Michael led me to a smooth fallen log; and we sat together, admiring the enchanting oasis before us. I was sitting on the edge of a large patch of marijuana but couldn't really see it for what it was. Just as I was wondering exactly what I was supposed to be looking at, Michael extended his arms and said, "So, what do you think?"

To an untrained and unsuspecting eye, the pot was difficult to distinguish from its natural surroundings. The plants blended into the hillside; all of the big fan leaves had turned the color of fall in the bush—yellow with tinges of brown and green. It took a minute to register; and I finally answered, "Oh, you're growing pot. God, it's so hard to see it there." I walked through the patch carefully, studying the tall, stinky plants. "So, you lied. You are a pot grower."

I let it sink in. Now, I knew what Michael had really been doing all this time at his forest retreat, why he was so strong and suntanned. He had spent the majority of his days that summer packing water to the clearing filled with marijuana plants. I understood why he hadn't told me at first, and I thought it a wise approach to cultivating something illegal.

That was the first time I'd ever seen a marijuana patch, although Michael's pot wasn't the first I'd seen growing—just the first I'd seen growing properly. I did have a vague memory of some marijuana plants my parents had grown as a horticultural experiment on their hobby farm. I had probably been about eight years old and hadn't paid much attention as my mother was always growing something new. Her repertoire of Latin names and new plant species was overwhelming for most adults. I paid almost no attention to her fledgling pot patch.

My mother is an extreme gardener. By this I mean that gardening is her life, and she will sacrifice anything for it. She has tried cultivating everything—if it can be grown in Canada, she's probably attempted it and likely had success. Somehow, in the early 1970's, she acquired a handful of marijuana seeds and planted them in with her corn, just to see what would happen.

The plants grew big and healthy, like the rest of her garden, on a steady diet of compost, manure, spring water and various kinds of organic mulch. Although monstrous, I'm sure these plants had very low potency because neither of my parents knew anything about pot. My dad cut it down prematurely and hung it in the barn until it was bone dry. Then, he smashed the living shit out of it with a broom, destroying all the buds and leaving only mounds of crispy leaves. This was loaded into the back of the family pickup and delivered to our "hippie" neighbors, a young couple notorious for their mass consumption of cannabis. They had agreed to take my parents' trial crop as payment for looking after our farm while we went on holidays. Satisfied with her experiment, my mother never grew another pot plant.

I only remember seeing the plants a few times that summer; but now, as a seasoned grower, I'm sure they had very little yield. Without a proper strain and appropriate cultivation techniques, pot plants will not necessarily produce buckets of mind-blowing smoke.

This time, with Michael's patch, I was getting my first look at some very healthy, sticky, ready-to-harvest pot. I thought it was beautiful. I found nothing offensive about it, and I couldn't believe that pot was illegal. Would my mother have been sent to jail for her gardening experiment? With three young children and a farm full of animals to care for, would she have been thrown in the back of a police car and read her rights for growing some experimental seeds in her corn patch?

There must be some mistake with this particular law, I thought. *Maybe someone wrote it down wrong, and the error just needs to be pointed out and corrected.* To me, these plants were just another flower growing among the ferns and trees in the middle of nowhere. The only difference was that if I told the wrong person about it the man of my dreams could be in serious shit.

And so began my entrance into a world of lies and secrecy—the Pot World, we call it. Getting in was easy for me—effortless, in fact.

Michael will always fondly remember that first spring he decided to try his hand at growing. No one would have believed he'd be capable of nurturing any kind of crop to fruition. He'd never grown anything in his thirty-seven years of life. He'd been raised on a city lot, in a family whose main focus in life was the hotel and liquor business—a business he joined as soon as he could. This urban background hadn't prepared him for the cultivation of anything, except maybe relationships in the world of bars and hotels.

Michael's main focus had always been work, football, parties and, of course, girls. Not surprisingly, his entry to the Pot World came in a bar.

Michael and his cousin Jimmy had impulsively bought a hundred clones from a convincing friend in a strip bar...

* * *

"Hey, Mike, how're you doing?" The burly friend hugged Michael tightly and patted him on the back. "I heard you had a bad accident. You doing okay?"

"Yeah, man, I'm fine, almost as good as new. I fucked up my wrist pretty good but other than that, I can't complain." Michael demonstrated his almost useless right wrist and tried to laugh.

"That's a drag, Mike," the friend said earnestly. "Since you're not working and you've got that land out at the lake now, why don't you grow a crop of pot this summer? It'll really get you in touch with your land and keep you and psycho-cousin here out of trouble. I just happen to have an awesome strain, rooted and ready. Buddy just cancelled his order, and these girls need a good home."

Michael considered the proposition for a couple of minutes, consulted an inebriated Jimmy and said, "Sure. Why the hell not!"

* * *

Clones are rooted cuttings of a female plant or plants; and each has the potential to grow into a mature, bud-producing female. Male plants are not used because they produce pollen and contaminate the females with unwanted seeds. Most outdoor clones are worth between ten and twenty dollars. The clones Michael acquired that night set him and Jimmy back a thousand dollars, and he really had no idea how to turn them into a viable crop.

The suggestion of growing pot as a way to make some money while getting in touch with his new piece of property and convalescing seemed nothing short of brilliant. Living in a bus on a secluded acreage without even the prospect of a job and having spent most of his savings, he decided to be adventurous and attempt one small crop. It seemed like the right thing to do. Surely, these plants would make him either spiritual or rich while nicely complementing his new lifestyle.

Michael had always secretly dreamed of a rustic life in the wilderness. He fantasized about living off the land and being self-sufficient. It was handy, of course, that his wealthy parents owned a summer home only a short drive from his wilderness paradise. That way, when the Mountain Man needed a hot shower, a little TV fix or a place to entertain his constant stream of exotic dancers, he had only to saddle up his old truck and head down the dusty trail to the family cabin. The summer was unfolding into nothing short of a dream.

The clones sat in Jimmy's dark basement for two weeks until Michael and his cousin finally had the courage to drive out to the bush and face the task of planting. Jimmy had agreed to do anything he could to help get Michael back on his feet. Together, the two men carefully took the sickly, light-deprived plants out of the car and set them in the tall grass behind Michael's bus. Then, they looked at each other and started to laugh. Small chuckles at first, developing into full-blown, pants-wetting hysterics.

"What the fuck are we doing?" one said to the other, and the laughter continued.

Jimmy lay down in the soft grass and propped himself up on his elbows to stare intently at the little plants. He raised his thick eyebrows and shook his head thoughtfully. Michael joined him on the ground and nonchalantly stroked the leaves of a few of the clones as he studied them.

"Mickey, can you believe that these tiny little things are actually going to turn into marijuana plants and come off? How do we even know it's pot? I think we might be stupider than we look," Jimmy worried aloud.

"It's pot, all right, Jimmy. Haven't you ever seen clones before? They don't need to turn into marijuana plants—they are. Don't worry, man; they'll come off."

Here were two men who had never so much as planted a potato on the verge of planting an illegal crop of marijuana. It was impossible to imagine the gangly little weeds sitting in Pepsi cups were going to grow up and produce a big bundle of easy money come fall.

The cultivation of pot was not as prevalent ten years ago as it is now. It was not yet British Columbia's number-one cottage industry, with an abundance of books and magazines and an Internet full of help and information for growers. Michael fumbled along and was blessed with the beginner's luck that sucks a lot of people into this business. The spindly little clones in the Pepsi cups grew into amazing, bud-laden marijuana plants. An old friend in Alberta who made a living buying and reselling pot would take it all and pay cash. With all of the major bases covered, Michael scored right off the bat.

That first beautiful crop I saw on the picturesque hillside produced twenty-six pounds of dried marijuana that eventually sold for over $50,000. To help get it ready for market, I spent the majority of my days off that October immersed in a pile of stinky, wet pot learning the fine art of clipping.

Michael had read about hanging the plants upside down on some sort of clothesline to send maximum THC to the buds. The drying room had to be dark and cool with fans circulating the chilly air. After twenty-four hours upside down, the plants could be clipped. I sat cross-legged on the hard cabin floor in the same long underwear for a week. My fingers had big red sores and ridges where the scissors cut into my hands, but I persevered; and after only a few days I became an expert. I felt quite like the miller's daughter in the fable of Rumpelstiltskin—a lone damsel hidden away in a dark room, visited only by a greedy king who expects to have his mountain of straw spun into gold.

But my king wasn't really greedy. He was caring and appreciative, and we enjoyed the hours spent alone together turning the pot mountain into bundles of cash.

Clipping, grooming or *cleaning* refers to the removal of most of the leaves and stalk from each plant. It's tedious work, akin to mild torture; the job has only one or two moves, which are repeated at top speed thousands of times. The large branches containing many individual buds are broken down into smaller sections and trimmed with scissors. The desirable end result is a multitude of individual buds containing just enough leaf to protect them from falling apart.

These buds are then cut off the stalks and set somewhere to cure and dry. The trimmed leaf is referred to as "shake" and has some value, but is generally discarded or saved to make into oil. Buyers don't want to pay for unnecessary stalk or leaf because the pot is sold by weight, so a clean, presentable product is necessary.

Since we were novices, Michael's virgin crop was sculptured— over-groomed for outdoor pot—a work of art, we were told. Our buyer laughed ardently when we described our detailed harvesting and clipping techniques. He was very impressed but recommended we not work that hard again. We could have spent less than half the time clipping and still had a marketable product worth the same amount.

I was crushed when I heard this. I had put in fourteen to eighteen hours a day, leaving every joint in my body aching and stiff. The smell of pot penetrated my skin and hung around me for days, and my fingers were contorted and leper-like with open scabs and pus. This was only the first in a long line of lessons we would learn in the next ten years.

When I returned to work, I could hardly lift Doug out of bed because I had actually strained the muscles in my chest and arms with infinite hours of scissor work. Michael had no such complaints. He was enjoying success. He proudly named his product "Green Poodle" for its sculptured appearance and gave away Baggies of the manicured pot with homemade swizzle sticks carved out of dried stalks. After running far worse businesses with little or no financial success in an unpleasant milieu, Michael saw growing pot as his road to salvation.

* * *

SEPTEMBER 9, 2000—I called our lawyer, Tommy Dodge, from jail, and he told me to keep my mouth shut. "Don't say a fucking thing to anyone, Mary-Ann" were his exact words of advice. "The only one you should be talking to is me. I called Mike; he knows everything, I told him you'd be fine. He'll be there to pick you up as soon as you're released. Did you talk to anyone yet? Did you give a statement?"

"No." I said quietly. I told him I hadn't been asked to give a formal statement, but that I had admitted the pot was mine.

"That, my dear, is unfortunate but try not to worry. I'll look after it. And call me back if you need anything. It's your right to call me, and don't let them tell you otherwise. You should be out of there soon; Michael will pick you up and take you home. Call me tomorrow."

So, I clammed up and lay down on the skin-colored vinyl pad that matched the walls of my cell. Tired, achy and snot-ridden, I called to the matron on duty and demanded to be let out or given another phone call after waiting for several hours while the arresting officers did their paperwork.

YEAR TWO, 1993

Motherhood

JANUARY 16—*I looked at my reflection in the mirror: pale, gaunt and miserable. There are dark, brownish-purple rings under my eyes and my clothes sag like an anorexic hobo's. My breasts are almost nonexistent under a T-shirt that would fit a ten-year-old. What the hell has happened to me?*

My job and the endless hours of commuting to Michael's were slowly driving me to insanity; I had developed serious insomnia and weighed just over a hundred pounds.

Doug had been overjoyed when I left Craig and thought it was obvious he and I would make the perfect couple. We already kind of lived together, and he would never find a girl better at understanding him or caring for him. Doug couldn't share my happiness over my second chance with Michael and cringed whenever I mentioned his name. I loved Doug from the bottom of my heart but not in the kind of way he was hoping. Working together had become somewhat of a struggle for both of us.

I no longer slept nights at work and spent a lot of time wishing I could leave the city and never go back. I lived for the daily phone calls that Michael and I shared, always ending with both of us sad and missing each other. With much gut-wrenching guilt and relief, I finally told Doug that I didn't think I was mentally or physically fit enough to care for him. He actually agreed.

I made arrangements to move back to my parents' farm, about an hour's drive from Camp Hokenson. Although madly in love with Michael, I wasn't crazy enough to formally move in with him.

* * *

MARCH 1 —*Moving back home with my parents was my tonic; I've gained a few pounds and sleep peacefully every night. Every week I spend two or three days on the family farm and then drive out to see Michael. His bus isn't winterized, so he has temporarily moved into his parents' summer cabin on the lake. It feels weird to not go to work every day, but I'm so happy to be sleeping! My intense attraction to Michael is not wearing off; in fact, it seems to be getting stronger. I feel as if I could not live without this man, a dangerous state of being.*

Visiting at the cabin was a riot. The floors were knee-deep in papers, magazines, Chinese takeout containers, junk from garage sales and all kinds of clothing. And Michael always had something to show me—something he'd just spent his last ten dollars on—like an old liquor decanter with a paint-chipped ballerina inside or a musty book detailing the sexual cycles of vertebrates. We'd lie around the cabin, going through junk or watching movies, and go for walks along the lake when the weather permitted. By the end of March, I'd been home for four weeks…and my period was late.

* * *

MARCH 27—*There was no mistaking the color of the paper—it was blue. Oh, my God, I'm pregnant! Shit! How can this be? What's happening to my life? I feel out of control. I've been impregnated by an unemployed pot grower. I'm 28 years old and living in my parents' basement. Shit! I'm sure it won't*

> *amount to anything, but, my God! I wonder how*
> *Michael will take the news.*

This was certainly not something we had planned. Michael and I had talked about a future together, but it hadn't included children—I had assured him I was practically sterile and that the future would create itself. Michael calmly looked at me and said that if I wanted to have a baby he'd love to have one with me, but if I wanted to have an abortion he'd completely understand and support me in either decision. And after this he said, "Total fucking godhead," his own sacred phrase to prove that he, the constant fibber, was speaking the gospel truth.

I did have a history of obstetrical problems, so I wasn't going to allow myself to become too concerned with the issue of parenthood. I didn't believe I was capable of carrying a baby to term. Over the years, I'd undergone six obstetrical surgeries; I had only one ovary and, after several miscarriages, had pretty much resigned myself to a life without children.

So, Michael and I made a deal. If "it" was alive by the time we went for a three-month ultrasound, then it was meant to be; and we would rise to the occasion. Until such time, there was no point in worrying about something that was out of our control. We continued dating as usual and talked about the pregnancy as little as possible. I secretly thought about the life that might be growing inside me and couldn't help thinking that the kid would be amazing.

* * *

> MAY 29—*I lay in bed quietly, wondering how much*
> *my life would change after today. Everything looked*
> *the same outside the window I had broken with a*
> *tennis ball when I was nine. I squeezed my eyes shut*
> *and tried to transport myself back in time. Back to*
> *being young, safe with my parents and sisters, with*
> *my whole life ahead of me and my only*
> *responsibility a cat with a rash on her head. The*

phone rang and ended my teleportation.

I felt sick and nervous. Morning sickness was overtaking my body. The heat that I normally loved mixed with a multitude of smells made me nauseous and edgy. Michael arrived early, and I instantly felt a bit better. He squeezed my hand all the way to the hospital and cried when they told us "it" had a heartbeat.

Our respective parents had finally met to hear the results of our ultrasound. We called them together on my parent's lawn and blurted out the good news. Michael's mother, a strong Roman Catholic, asked why we hadn't used a condom. My mother said she hoped we didn't have any crazy ideas about her babysitting or knitting little booties—that would take time away from gardening. My dad was thrilled and said he hoped it was a girl, and Michael's father is insane and I can't remember what he said. That was the start of a long, sickly pregnancy for all of us.

The impending child made Michael more determined to grow pot, and plenty of it, to support his new family. His second year, to which we'd hardly given any serious thought until now, would have to far surpass the first; but he knew the two of us couldn't do it alone.

Things went as they inevitably do with Michael: he starts out small, succeeds at something and then dreams of going huge. With me pregnant and both of us basically unemployed, we needed a partner. After a brief discussion we decided that Cousin Jimmy was the ultimate candidate.

Jimmy was a very complex character. His mother, Michael's mother's sister, had beaten him as a child; and Jimmy was deeply emotionally scarred. His father ended up a skid row alcoholic, living on the street, drinking things like Lysol and vanilla. Jimmy also had a history of trouble with the bottle. He never finished high school but became a logger in northern B.C. Actually, he became a legend. He was ruggedly handsome, tougher than just about any guy you'll ever meet; and his logging abilities equaled his ability to piss off police, drink astounding amounts of liquor and basically act like a maniac. For example, he personally rolled eleven vehicles before the age of thirty.

At the same time, Jimmy possessed an amazing sense of humor and shared our intense love of animals and wilderness. He didn't conform to laws or rules, his incredible strength would come in handy and he had the necessary fulltime job to fund the coming year's activities. In short, Cousin Jimmy would be the perfect partner, and I was completely in awe of him.

Jimmy paid for gas, dirt, fertilizer, clones and booze. Michael provided the land and was responsible for maintenance labor throughout the season and a reliable buyer at the end of the year. Michael's years of clean living ended, too. He and his cousin needed to be in the same (altered) headspace to properly bond while tending the crop.

We all shared in the preparation of areas and the actual planting.

"Princess, your main job is to find suitable material to camouflage the holes. Look for leaves and twigs that can cover the dirt around the holes so they don't look so obvious."

I crawled through the bush on my hands and knees looking for anything that I could carry back to the holes Jimmy and Michael had dug with shovels and pickaxes. It had rained for days, giving the ground a snot-like consistency and making it difficult to gather anything that wasn't rotten. Bugs swarmed around my head, stinging and biting me anywhere there was exposed skin, the sheer number of them amazing. There was no relief from the persistent plague, and I finally just gave up and let them have me.

"Just who, exactly, are we hiding the holes from, Master?" I asked sarcastically, the cloud of mosquitoes above my head driving me to the brink of madness. "There isn't a soul for miles, and since when is it illegal to dig holes on your own land? Why all the fuss?" I demanded.

"The camouflage, my grumpy little princess, is for helicopters. If anyone flew over here they'd see hundreds of great big empty brown holes, and they'd probably figure out just what was going in them. But you've done enough for today; you can stop any time you like. We'll come back tomorrow, and Jimmy and I'll finish up. Jimmy! Let's get going, cousin."

As Michael explained his reasoning to me, Jimmy had

23

disappeared into a newly dug hole, the combination of alcohol and greasy mud too much, even for a skilled bushman.

The days turned into weeks as the pristine property took on the look of a war zone. By mid-June we were ready for planting and eagerly anticipating the completion of our gardening project. All we needed now were clones; but fate stepped in, ruining our plans, changing everything. It also devastated the family of the guy supplying our clones—he had his legs squashed in some kind of freak accident and had to be hospitalized.

The three of us sat, despondent, staring at the huge pile of baled dirt, bags of expensive fertilizer, forty acres of water line, five hundred cavernous holes dug by a drunken Cousin Jimmy—and no marijuana plants. By now, it was the end of June; and most growers had already finished planting.

"What the hell are we going to do, cousin?" Jimmy asked, raising his cooler to the sky.

"We'll have to put together some more money and find someone with babies for sale. I've got a couple more buddies who owe me— someone'll come through."

Being new to the game, we had no mother plants to cut clones from; and none of us knew anyone else who would have outdoor clones for sale, especially this late in the season. We couldn't take out an ad in the local farming paper so, finally, a desperate Michael phoned the distraught wife of the recently squished clone supplier. She told him to fuck off.

Ashamed but resourceful, Michael eventually found three hundred-eighty suitable clones. We finished planting in late July, one month behind schedule.

I struggled to keep up with Cousin Jimmy as we climbed the trail leading to the main patch.

"Mary-Ann, hand me that bag of blue shit." Jimmy gestured to a pile of fertilizer sacks wedged under a tree with his enormous right hand.

"Let me mix it today, Jimmy. I think they like the higher doses we've been giving them. Look how huge they all are! I always knew that more was better." Jimmy threw me a half-empty bag of 20-20-20 and sat down on a wide stump to enjoy some kind of purple alcoholic beverage he'd just discovered.

"You're right, and I like your style. That boyfriend of yours has got to quit babying these goddamned weeds; he's like an old mother hen, fussing and worrying. Can you believe he uses those little tiny measuring spoons? He's like a mad scientist with his blond curls sticking out all over and the little tiny spoons putting in the little tiny fertilizer. Meanwhile, it's me and you that are going to make these weeds grow. We'll tell old Mickey what we've been up to when he sees how good the crop is this year. Throw another handful in for good luck there, cousin."

Jimmy's motives were a mystery to me; what kept him in this partnership? He had never cared about money, and he didn't really like the plants or give a shit about how they turned out. In fact, that was pretty much how he felt about life in general. He referred to the plants only as "weeds" or "hippie shit" and would purposely step on tender young leaves, stems and branches. He was only in it to wander around in the bush and drink beer and coolers with his cousins.

Michael, on the other hand, was falling in love with growing pot and everything that went with it. He loved being outside all day and breathing fresh air. He loved being his own boss and sharing his workspace with birds and animals instead of drunk people. I, too, enjoyed growing, for the experience of the process as well as the financial rewards. I honestly believed that the more food I poured into the plants, the better they would be; and this, in turn, would make Michael proud and happy. I continued to over-fertilize, and the plants continued to co-operate.

We awoke together to only the sound of wind working its way through the treetops. Birds called out to each other and crickets sang in the grass as we lay in the darkened bedroom of the bus. I felt as if there could be no happier person alive on the planet as Michael snuggled against my back, lightly rubbing my growing belly. We had no phone, no running water and an obligation only to the pot plants.

A loud knock on the side of the bus shattered the tranquil morning; Cousin Jimmy was out for the weekend.

"Hey, you two! What are you doing in there? You better be careful,

Mary-Ann, or he'll get you pregnant."

Michael and I hurried out of the bus, and the three of us made plans for the day. It was overcast, so Michael chose to take advantage of the weather and put in a patch of oversized plants.

"Chopper! Total fucking godhead, run for cover!" Michael yelled as we'd barely reached the edge of the patch.

A helicopter flew over us, low and deafening. It circled the patch momentarily, ruffling the trees and churning up dust before heading to the north side of the property. We automatically dove for cover under an old cedar tree when we heard the roar and Michael's warning. Michael grabbed watering jugs and hoses and flung them deep into the underbrush. I grabbed the biggest plant I could carry and tripped over an exposed root, dropping the plant and my pregnant self clumsily under the protective branches of the tree.

Our plants were so small that they couldn't be seen from the air; but it was a police chopper, and it was flying low. When the dust settled and the helicopter moved on, we noticed our dear cousin Jimmy had grabbed nothing but his six-pack of beer. The look on Jimmy's face as he realized what he had saved made us all laugh hysterically. His crooked grin erupted into a snicker as he apologized for not being more helpful. The big, muscular bushman had no instinctive concern for the crop. It became more apparent as the year wore on that booze was truly Jimmy's reason for living.

Jimmy's worsening addiction to alcohol wasn't exactly a news flash. A few weeks before the helicopter incident he got so drunk that he drove ten miles out of town before realizing he desperately needed a washroom. He was in no condition to find a public toilet so he stopped his car, pulled down his jeans, filled his underwear and threw them into the ditch, cargo and all. He'd always do objectionable stuff like this and then tell us about it the next day. We found his candor endlessly amusing but wondered if he'd ever ease up on the drinking before he got into serious trouble.

A few weeks later, on a muggy Sunday afternoon, we went to Jimmy's house to see why he'd missed a weekend of work. He looked pale, disheveled and depressed. He then quite seriously announced that he had quit drinking for good. Michael and I looked at each other, shocked, and asked what monumental event had brought on such a drastic decision. He proceeded to tell us his honest and embarrassing motive.

"Last night I went to the bar; and, somehow, I got inebriated. I picked up this girl I met and brought her home for the night. Now, she was no supermodel—in fact, she was actually just a gross pig when you come right down to it." Jimmy laughed at the memory and then shuddered a little. "But hey, she was good enough for a night of loving. She was drunk, too, and more than willing to have dear old Jimmy; but she told me she wouldn't fuck a guy like me without a condom."

Jimmy paused for dramatic effect; and, finally, we pulled the rest of the story out of him.

Condoms were something Jimmy didn't exactly have stockpiled. The room was spinning and Jimmy's hormones raging as he blindly stumbled into the kitchen, wrapped a liberal amount of plastic wrap around his drunken dick and seduced the wanton damsel. Later, he got up to poop and threw up on himself while sitting on the toilet, the piece of plastic wrap still stuck to his thigh. It was at this exact moment that Jimmy decided the drink might be getting the best of him.

My cheeks hurt from laughing, and Michael sat slapping his thigh with tears streaming down his face. The thought of Jimmy parading through his modest little house with its clean, white walls and new gray carpet with a chunk of plastic wrap stuck to his penis was just too much. We stayed to visit for a few more hours to hear more of the grisly details. By the time we left, Jimmy was up, dressed and drinking his third or fourth cooler of the day. He planned on heading to a golf tournament sponsored by his favorite pub. That was the only time I ever knew Cousin Jimmy to quit drinking.

Another day, Jimmy arrived late to work, nursing a wicked hangover. There was a hornets' nest near the start of our trail, and we all knew it was there and took care to avoid it. On this particular day, Jimmy informed us that it was really no big deal to be stung by insects.

"With hornets, or any other little insects with stingers, there really isn't any pain if you can realize it's all in your head. You just remain calm and..." He approached the buzzing nest armed with a long stick and poked and swatted until the angry occupants emerged. "See?"

Michael and I ran far enough away to avoid being stung but stayed within viewing distance out of morbid curiosity. Jimmy's broad, shirtless back was quickly black with hornets, as were his head and arms and hands. He cautiously ran a hand over his face to clear his eyes and ears of the swarming insects. As he slowly turned to face us, we noticed one lone hornet hanging nonchalantly off his cheek, stinger fully engaged. He trudged towards us, smiling, arms outstretched, legs marching stiffly like a horror show character. Once again, Michael and I were doubled over laughing; and the harder we laughed the more abuse the nest received from cousin Jimmy's stick.

The three of us ran, spastically trying to avoid the hornets but loving the adrenaline and adventure all the same. When the show was over a few minutes later we all continued up the path to work. Jimmy was completely unaffected by his multitude of stings. Within about twenty minutes, all the welts subsided; and he casually put his shirt back on. Maybe, in some ways, he was smarter than people thought.

Six months into my pregnancy, I got my divorce and severed the last ties to my old life in the city. I did help with the crop whenever possible, but I also spent a lot of that summer in the hospital.

* * *

AUGUST 24—*I'm so scared. There's so much bleeding every time I move—bright red, like paint. I don't know how a baby could survive in such a compromised womb; I'm already failing this child and it hasn't yet been born. I feel strongly that the baby is small and deformed, a wrinkled little alien with eight fingers on each hand, covered in slime. I wish I could see inside myself to be better prepared.*

True to form, I had a potentially life-threatening condition called *placenta praevia.* I bled constantly and was meant to be resting in bed, but I disobeyed my doctor at every turn. It was so difficult for an active person in the honeymoon phase of a new relationship to stay home in bed—alone. Finally, the doctor told us that we had to come in from our remote rural camp and move to within five minutes of a hospital. My pregnancy was high-risk, and he said he'd refuse to care for me if I wouldn't follow his instructions.

We made the move in September, days before my twenty-ninth birthday. I had just been discharged from a difficult five-day stay in the hospital. For about a week, we lived in a sterile ground-floor motel room on the outskirts of town, until we found a suitable house to rent. It was hideous but close to the hospital, so our doctor and our families were happy. I, on the other hand, was totally depressed because I was stuck in bed and no longer part of the crew or the action. Michael and Jimmy went to work every day while I sat in the decorator's nightmare on a dead-end street.

Never before had I occupied a home that was so utterly devoid of character—three identical boxes joined together by a continuous set of stairs. Every wall in every room was white, and the large square windows had no blinds or curtains. The carpet was off-white with the odd stain left by former tenants. Forbidden to move around, I was powerless to change a thing. Michael showered me with food and gifts of every variety and was usually home in time to tuck me into bed. He never missed one doctor's appointment and did his best to cheer me up and convince me that I wasn't missing anything by staying home. Most days, I lay on the couch eating and eagerly awaiting the birth of the child I was now convinced must be an alien.

* * *

SEPTEMBER 21—*Michael has called in his old friend Herman to "professionally" assess the crop. We agreed on wanting everything done right—from harvesting at peak time to following all the proper steps for clipping and curing. This year's crop will not be over-groomed or dried too quickly, and*

*Herman has been hired to guide us. Michael
promises that, although maybe a touch eccentric,
Herman loves and understands marijuana
passionately.*

An old, rust-eaten green truck arrived laden with boxes and bundles
and a slender, dark driver. I peered through the window, anxious to
catch my first glimpse of our savior. Michael referred to Herman as a
young Frank Zappa on acid, and it wasn't hard to see why. His thick,
longish hair was as dark as charcoal, and his eyes were soft and
intelligent. An expansive moustache covered most of his cheeks and
completely obscured his teeth. As he approached the front door, I
noticed his raunchy T-shirt and satchel of books and newspaper
clippings.

I extended my hand to Herman, but he stepped towards me and
hugged me like a long-lost friend. His smile was quick and genuine,
and he started laughing as he stepped back to examine Michael and
me. Through bloodshot and partly closed eyes, Herman pronounced
us an exceptional couple.

Herman was brilliant and a connoisseur of many drugs, including
and especially marijuana; his consumption over the past three
decades had been nothing short of miraculous. Michael and I were
glad to have him on board. We welcomed Herman into our humble
home, and I left the two old friends alone to catch up.

Herman would go out into the patch every day with a magnifying
glass, notepad, walking stick and camera and check the crystal
formation on the ripest plants...

* * *

"Michael, come and take a look at this." Herman stood back from
the plant he was examining and took a long drag of his joint. "This is
what the crystals should look like when the plant is optimum for
harvest. It's very important not to disturb the crystals; just look
carefully. When the tops have these little balls formed on the tips of
them, your THC concentration is at its highest. The top of this plant is

ready."

Thirsty for knowledge, Michael stared in awe at what the powerful scope revealed, drinking in all the new information. The *crystals* referred to in marijuana cultivation are gooey balls that form on the top of tiny stems that cover the buds and inner leaves. In this resinous substance are the psychoactive chemicals—mainly THC—that produce the marijuana high. When the crystals are clearly round balls poised atop individual stems, the pot is at its peak.

Most outdoor crops aren't harvested with the aid of a microscope. It's obvious to the naked eye when pot is ripe and ready to come down. But Michael wanted things done Herman's way because this year's crop was to be perfect.

After painstakingly harvesting only the ripest plants, Herman ordered me to start cutting tiny holes in dozens of cardboard boxes and run strings through them to hang the clipped buds on. I made enough of these ridiculous boxes to realize it was not the way to dry a large quantity of pot, and I had the audacity to say so.

"Hey, Herman, I'm not doing this anymore. It's a stupid idea, okay? Where do you expect me to put all of these boxes? I think you're being a bit obsessive for an outdoor crop of this size. Just leave me alone, please."

Admittedly bitchy, I knew he would chalk my refusal up to pregnancy or hormones; but I didn't care about anything anymore. I was completely burned out. Herman was miffed and sighed melodramatically, disappointed in my work.

The tiny bedroom we were using for drying had screens built from floor to ceiling on one side, attached to the wall with heavy screws. Bags of pot lay in the middle of the room and my body and supplies filled the doorway. Jimmy and Michael had emptied every cardboard box we owned, and I still had only enough room to dry a couple of pounds Herman's way. It took longer to locate a box and rig it with the tiny clotheslines than it had to sculpt last year's crop.

Michael sided with me and told Herman to concentrate on harvesting rather than drying. The buds were really starting to add up, and it was all I could do to get through the piles without the pot wilting or molding—Herman would have to get over it.

Herman also took offense at people "disturbing the crystals," which led to endless ridicule of him behind his back. Jimmy would throw bags of pot on the clipping room floor and jump up and down on it, saying, "What do you think Herman would think of this? Huh? Stupid, fucking hippie. Wouldn't want to *disturb the crystals*. I'll show him disturbed crystals. That little runt of a man is disturbed himself."

Cousin Jimmy couldn't stand Herman and thought he was nothing more than a dirty, lazy hippie. I was growing tired of the obsessive, repetitive rhetoric and joined Jimmy in squashing all the crystals I could find.

No one was shocked when Herman quit prematurely. Spit squeezed through his tawny teeth as he told us, "None of you people are serious enough! You have no respect for the spirituality of marijuana. It isn't about money and production...or speed. It's about quality and cannabinoids!"

He packed up his tired old truck, gathered up bags of free clippings and shake and turned in his hours. The final tally included twenty hours for "analysis" and a separate charge for danger pay.

Jimmy said under his breath, "Don't forget your dope, there, Herman, on your way out, you lazy-shit hippie" as Herman piled the last garbage bag into the cab of his truck.

Michael thanked Herman profusely and assured him he'd do his best to whip us into shape. As soon as the truck was out of sight, we all burst into unrestrained, delirious laughter.

People in the Pot World usually don't fit into society very well. Guys like Herman are common in the drug business—I just didn't know it yet. I took for granted the six precious months spent among "normal" people in an actual neighborhood. Nor did I know that the ugly house on the dead-end street would represent my last daily contact with the real world for many years.

A long, hot summer and massive doses of fertilizer helped our three hundred-eighty plants grow into a crop of one hundred-ten pounds. The next hurdle was finding a safe place where we could process the bulk of the large, stinky plants. We had started clipping at home simply for convenience, always planning on finding a suitable clip house. But the ripening pot couldn't wait. Suddenly, every plant we had was mature, and fall was slipping away. Desperate, rushed and lacking a better alternative, Michael and Jimmy ultimately hauled the entire crop of '93 sixty-five miles to our newly rented house.

We had close neighbors on both sides, which made dumping the steaming bags of dope a dicey undertaking. All deliveries were made in the dark, either early in the morning before five or at night after midnight. The contents of the tiny bedroom soon spilled into the hallway and took over one complete level of the house. There, we sat and clipped for a full six weeks, aided by our newest employee.

Sherry Taylor was an old friend of Michael's who had worked for him at one of his nightclubs during the bar years. Although they hadn't worked together in years, Michael and Sherry had always kept in touch and helped each other out with life's little obstacles. She was a single mother of two and hadn't had a fulltime job for over a year. She was also an avid gardener and lover of all plants, marijuana included.

Sherry had long, thick hair the color of sand and the whitest teeth I had ever seen. She was tall, slim and muscular; her attire always included a flower-print "gardening dress," a pair of sandals and an oversized purse that weighed about twenty pounds. In a world where it's hard to find trustworthy, available people willing to work long hours in sticky, stinky conditions, Sherry was a godsend. She was dedicated, friendly and quickly became an expert clipper. She also became a dear friend to me. Her company made the monotonous job of clipping pot bearable, and our days were spent gossiping and laughing as we groomed the seemingly endless deluge of dope.

* * *

OCTOBER 25—*It was overcast and raining all day. Most of the trees have dropped their leaves while ghosts sway and pumpkins glow on every second porch. The smell of wet pot has enveloped our house like a shroud and permeated the entire neighborhood. I am scheduled for a routine prenatal visit, a welcome break from clipping.*

"Mary-Ann, you make sure to give your hair a good dousing of perfume—right before you leave the house, honey," advised Sherry. "Even when you think you're clean and you've had a shower, your hair probably just reeks. Mine stinks for two days after a clip."

I took Sherry's advice and sprayed myself liberally: hair, clothes, skin—everywhere. With a new outfit on, I felt confident and composed as I drove across the bridge that led to my doctor.

At my doctor's office, the nurse weighed me, took my blood pressure and requested a urine sample. She then showed me to an empty examining room, where I gazed at my substantial reflection in a small mirror above the sink. Only my head still seemed to belong to me; the thick midsection I'd been growing looked out-of-place on my thin, straining legs.

When the doctor arrived a few minutes later, he started sniffing the air with a muddled look on his young face.

"Do you smell skunk?" he asked, honestly puzzled.

Horrified, I said that I had a bad cold and couldn't smell anything. After all, how could a skunk get loose in a city and stink up a doctor's office? I guess I could have said that I hit one on the highway; but, at the time, I was sure he knew the smell was coming from me. I made it through the rest of the visit imagining POT GROWER tattooed on my forehead in big black letters. I loved and respected my doctor and hoped he wouldn't think any less of me as I slunk out of his office.

Neither Michael nor I smoked marijuana and—even though we grew it and sold it—at that time, I worried about the stigma of being labeled a "pot smoker." I wanted my doctor to know how serious I was about being healthy during my pregnancy. I didn't smoke anything, yet I drove home feeling stupid and ashamed. Within minutes, I had my work clothes back on and a skunky-smelling marijuana tree draped over my lap. Stigma or not, I was part of the Pot World now, and I had work to finish.

Our rented house was directly above a low-end strip bar and a by-the-month hotel frequented by winos. There was plenty of pedestrian traffic and close neighbors on both sides; but, somehow, we managed to get away with clipping, drying and selling over a hundred pounds of pot without a single hitch.

The neighbors directly beside us to the west had a rental suite in their basement, and their tenant—an Elvis impersonator—regularly came to our door wanting to use our telephone. He'd come over in full costume, looking utterly absurd, and go on and on about his latest karaoke contest. I wanted nothing more than to tell him to get lost and pay for his own fucking phone calls, but I couldn't—he may have smelled pot and could have turned us in for revenge if we cut off his phone privileges. Michael told me that we had to let him in and to act like we had nothing to hide.

This was my first lesson in being nice to everyone, no matter how I really felt about them, because I was doing something illegal. People who live in pot houses, just like those in glass houses, can't afford to throw any stones.

Sherry and I clipped in a room directly above the street that was intended as the baby's nursery. I wasn't due till the end of December; this was early November, and we figured we had lots of time to do our work before my due date. The pot kept coming—day after day, bag after bag with no end in sight. On November 11, I started bleeding worse than usual; we deemed it serious enough for me to go back to the hospital. I was never happier to check myself in. I abandoned my loyal partner and had an emergency caesarean section that night.

* * *

NOVEMBER 12—*Suddenly, I am a mother. Nothing has prepared me for how much I love the tiny little creature that is our daughter. Her name is Daisy, and every time I look at her I cry. She is perfect, not an alien thing about her. The only sad thing is that the love of my life is not here. My stomach aches from being cut open, and I'm weak from loss of blood and sleep. But it's finally over, and everything is fine.*

Michael wasn't there for the onerous birth of our child. He'd left town to sell forty pounds of pot after the doctor assured him there was no way our baby would be born that prematurely. He returned the next day and, after he recovered from the shock and joy of the baby's arrival, told me about the sales trip that almost went bad.

It started with the packaging. Michael and Cousin Jimmy had set out for Edmonton with their merchandise wrapped in Ziploc freezer bags. Each bag was placed inside another bag with a sprinkling of baby powder in between. Someone had recommended this; and, as far as we can tell, it worked for the first several hours.

The long drive was uneventful, and the tired cousins checked into a motel room for the night. But Jimmy got a surprise when he left their room early the following morning.

He woke Michael with a grin and said, "Cousin Mickey, I think you'd better come out here a minute."

The frost-covered parking lot was alive with the smell of marijuana. The baby powder had obviously been overpowered during the night, and the skunky aroma of pot was seeping from the trunk. The cousins bumped up their meeting time with the buyer and hastily checked out of the motel. Within a few hours, the stinky pot was replaced with a tidy bundle of money, and Jimmy and Michael went shopping to celebrate. They hit the West Edmonton Mall in a frenzy and shopped until their feet hurt and they knew it was time to head home.

Halfway home, a snowstorm developed, forcing another night in a motel. Jimmy hid the money under a chair cushion in their room, and the weary shoppers bedded down. Early the next morning, Jimmy hurried outside into the freezing November rain to warm up the car while Michael checked out at the front desk. Jimmy left the car and headed back to the room to finish packing and grab the bags.

With the engine running and no one in sight, I guess the old beater looked pretty warm and inviting. Michael was chatting with the man behind the front desk as the clerk glanced out the window over Michael's shoulder and asked him if he knew the scruffy-looking guy behind the wheel of Jimmy's car. Before Michael could even answer, Jimmy strolled outside carrying the cousins' suitcases and shopping bags. As he approached his car, it slowly clunked into reverse. The would-be car thief saw Jimmy and panicked, backing into a wall of the motel. Jimmy slammed the bags onto the hood of his car and raced back into the motel after the fleeing thief.

Panicking, the man ran up a flight of stairs but came quickly back down, pleading with the front desk clerk for help. The clerk refused to cooperate and instead pointed Jimmy in the direction of the would-be thief as he scrambled back up the stairs.

Jimmy began the ascent, each angry footstep more exaggerated than his last.

"So, you like my car, hotshot? You still want to take it?" Jimmy taunted the man, who was by now squatting in the corner, shaking hands wrapped over his head, begging not to be hurt.

Jimmy reached down and slapped the bandit hard across the side of his face, grinning as blood poured from a cut on the man's lip.

"I had some very valuable merchandise in that car, shithead. What gives you the right to take someone else's car? Huh?"

The man made no attempt to answer Jimmy's question and, instead, offered a string of muddled apologies. Jimmy kicked the guy square in the guts before slowly descending the staircase that lead to the lobby. The grateful cousins tipped the front desk clerk generously and turned Jimmy's old Impala towards home.

They had driven over twenty miles before Jimmy realized they'd left the money under the chair cushion in their hotel room—in all the excitement, they'd forgotten it entirely. Luckily, it was still there when they returned, giggling at each other for being so disorganized and careless. The rest of the trip home was uneventful—save for the surprise waiting for Michael in the hospital.

I was a mother and Michael a dad yet nothing changed at home—at least, not immediately. Our daughter couldn't come home from the hospital with me; she had to be tube-fed every three hours and monitored until she was strong enough to eat on her own. While she gained strength, we steam-cleaned and painted her room and moved the last of the drying pot to another bedroom. Pot has a way of taking over a home, much like a pet or a spoiled child. My laundry hampers were full of pot, as was every available large container in the house.

Every corner contained incriminating material of some kind, and the biggest job was making it all disappear.

Our premature but healthy baby girl came home ten days later. By now, all of the pot had been sold; and we had a lot of money.

After that, everything changed. Michael cried every time he looked at our new baby. Seven weeks premature, she was tiny and frail and beautiful. We took turns feeding her every three hours. I slept at night while Michael and the cats moved into Daisy's room for the quiet, nocturnal feedings. During the day, I was up early while Michael slept in; and, by noon, the three of us were all together. After two months, Daisy had gained more than the required amount of weight and was healthy and happy. Michael and I were both thrilled with parenthood and couldn't imagine how we ever lived without our precious little Daisy.

* * *

SEPTEMBER 9, 2000 — Specifically instructed by Constable Fat-Ass not to phone home, I did.

"Princess, are you okay? What's going on out there?" Michael knew I had been arrested because Tommy had called to tell him. As we discussed what had happened, I watched the evidence from our big bust being bagged.

One side of the phone room was Plexiglas, giving me a view into the back of the police station. I saw my wet bag of buds being weighed, sealed and labeled; and then I saw another bag being sealed, its odd-looking contents a temporary mystery. I finished my phone call and asked to be taken back to my cell. I was exhausted. It had been over five hours since our arrest, and I was starting to feel despondent. I wanted to go home.

After another hour or two, we were finally released. Mikayla was outside in the deserted parking lot, smoking a cigarette with cold, trembling hands. She was drained and exhausted, and her face was stained with mascara; but her huge blue eyes lit up when I approached her. We hugged each other and rocked back and forth, each apologizing to the other profusely. I wiped her face with my sleeve and assured her that everything would be just fine.

Mikayla was told she would not be charged with anything, but I had been charged with production of a controlled substance, possession of marijuana and possession for the purpose of trafficking. Mikayla was shaken and confused but in relatively good spirits. We exchanged stories about our respective nights, which left me angered at how she had been treated.

Most cops expect women to cry and spill their guts, and have an easy time intimidating them. Mikayla had been threatened with a year in prison and the confiscation of her car if she didn't cooperate. The police told her that Michael and I were huge "drug kingpins" in our community. She had been driven around and coerced into looking for "the grow house" while simultaneously being yelled at and then soothed with reassurances and free cigarettes.

While Mikayla was detained in a cell, Constable Stark had brought her a bag of drugs to identify.

"What is this? Is she selling them, too? Are they some kind of mushrooms?" He wanted to know what other weird substance I was peddling and thrust the bag under her nose for inspection. Mikayla laughed for the only time all night as she identified the remains of my lunch. He wanted to charge me with possession of organic lychee fruit.

The bottom of my lunch cooler had been filled with the shells as I devoured the bag on the way to the clip shack. The matron on duty couldn't believe that neither of the policemen on duty had ever seen lychee nuts. I had already started writing this book at the time of my second arrest and couldn't wait to include this story. Two B.C. cops with no idea that pot plants could be grown outdoors in September, and no knowledge of the difference between magic mushrooms and lychee nutshells. I felt safe and reassured knowing men like this were serving and protecting us all.

There was nothing I could do now but wait for my court appearance and try to forget about my latest arrest.

YEAR THREE, 1994

New Beginnings

JANUARY 7—*Last night I dreamed about being busted, and it scared the shit out of me. I thought I was ok with all this pot-growing criminal stuff, but I can't help thinking it's too easy, too good to be true. Someone's going to notice that we never go to work. And there's this "proceeds of crime" thing everyone is talking about—they can seize your car, your home, your children, apparently! Every time I talk to Michael about it, it's like he's not really listening. I've got a bad feeling that, eventually, something is going to happen.*

With the growing season over, we had the next few months off to be with our new baby and relax after a long, crazy year. A soft blanket of snow had covered the hills and trees as the cloak of winter thickened. But Michael couldn't relax. He never wanted to have to beg for clones again; so, to ensure a good supply of cuttings for the new year, he converted our laundry room to a grow room. The plants did well. In fact, they soon outgrew their allotted space, and the two-car garage started to look promising.

Even after my recent abdominal surgery, I was forced to park my brand-new vehicle outside on a steep, slippery incline two inches away from the warm, sheltered garage. If I fell and broke my neck on the ice, or if my flabby, newly sliced stomach ripped open (as I was always imagining it might), I suppose it would have been tragic; but at least the plants would be safe.

It was around this time that I really started to question the whole pot-producing thing and vocalize my concerns to Michael. I didn't want to be locked out of the garage all winter or have to lie to the landlord, who simply wanted to come and change the furnace filter. The house had started to stink again; there was always dirt and water being spilled everywhere. The money was nice, but it came with feelings of guilt and paranoia. So, we talked about going straight; and, for once, Michael listened.

Michael and Jimmy bought a large acreage overlooking the lake and made plans to develop the land. They had been eyeing up the property for months and had no excuses not to follow through with the project. This investment in a legitimate future made us all feel better. The land would be a partnership between the two cousins— and a way to bond and be together outside the Pot World.

The development property would not contain marijuana in any form. Michael could comfortably ease out of growing and into his own legitimate business. He even enrolled in a real estate course. Things looked promising.

Michael had decided not to grow with a partner ever again. He'd also decided that Cousin Jimmy wasn't cut out for the pot business. The two men were great friends but had completely different views on how to approach life and work. Michael had tired of the pointless boozing and was now focused on supporting his family. Unlike Jimmy, he saw pot growing as a business and not some drunken, part-time hobby. The purchase of the land would clean up drug money and give the two cousins a reason to spend productive time together.

In February, Michael spent the better part of a week sneaking around behind my back. At night he'd patrol the alleys for large, clean cardboard boxes, piling his old pickup to capacity. Having an excuse to look in dumpsters was exciting for the junk collector; and, of course, he came home with a lot more than cardboard. During the day, he locked himself in the basement, turning his findings into his own secret project. Bewildered, I feared the worst and was sure it had something to do with the almighty herb that was still running our lives.

February 14, Valentine's Day. I woke up at five in the morning and crept downstairs to the kitchen. I left Michael and Daisy snuggled together in our bed, both snoring lightly. I wiped the moisture off the windows with a handful of paper towel and leaned over the sink to look out.

Every house on the block was sprinkled with a light dusting of new snow; it was going to be a perfect day for romance. Sitting on the kitchen table was an elaborately decorated cardboard castle; I knew it must be for me. I carefully opened the top of the structure and peeked inside. There were gifts, pictures, notes and pieces of oddly shaped cardboard, each wrapped in a different type of bright-colored paper. As I started pulling the pieces out, I realized they were giant letters. It took me a while to decipher the message; but, once I had them all laid out, they spelled "Will You Marry Me?"

I sat at the table, digesting the present, and cried. Even though we had a child together, it was wonderful to know that our commitment to each other would soon be official. I said yes and accepted the rest of my Valentine's Day present.

During our daughter's first few months of life she blossomed. No longer a skinny premature baby, she was healthy enough for us to move back to the bush after four months of diligent feeding and love. We now had enough money for a down payment on a house, so we bought one. Or, I should say, Michael did. I never saw the house until we owned it. Michael bought it in the dark on a Sunday night; all he did was look through a few windows and note that it was large and sturdy and there were no immediate neighbors. The house was purchased mainly for its location and price.

It was the last house in a remote subdivision that never reached completion. A well-built split-level home with vaulted ceilings and a massive stone fireplace, it sat facing south, looking out over the lake at an elevation of over twenty-five hundred feet. The mile-and-a-half-long driveway required a four-wheel drive and guaranteed relative privacy. Of course there were no neighbors, and the place was surrounded by Crown land. It cost only $97,500, and the owner

42

offered to carry the financing; it was perfect.

* * *

> APRIL 1—*Moving day. I exuberantly said goodbye to the rental house and packed up the last few boxes of food and cleaning supplies. Sun streamed in through the living room windows as I vacuumed the carpets for the last time. Tonight I'll sleep in the first house I've ever owned and have a garden and kitchen of my own design. The three stray cats we have acquired and the two-car garage full of mother plants required some ingenious packing, but our move was smooth. One of Michael's first projects in the new house is accommodating the now ever-present marijuana.*

Sherry helped me clean and paint the two main levels of the house while the beautiful finished basement was converted to a grow room. Shelves were ripped out, hooks were hung in the ceilings, windows were blacked out and boarded up and wires ran everywhere. Once again, dirt and water covered the floors. And this was just the beginning. Soon, Michael would be cloning for the new season. He planned to go really big this year and make enough money to complete phase one of the land development project. His goal for the year was one thousand plants, and we'd already lined up live-in help. Sherry's son Tony, whom I'd met only twice, would join our family at the start of spring planting.

Michael had no time to help me with the new house and no time to be with Daisy.

"Why did we even bother getting married if we're never going to see each other?" I demanded. "You haven't so much as eaten a meal with us in almost a month; and, when we do see you, all you talk about is pot and how sore and tired you are. I'm sick of it! There is more to life than fucking pot plants, and I don't know why you can't see that! Is this how it's going to be, because if it is, I'm not interested!"

I demanded a response from Michael and waited for his answer.

"Have you ever owned your own business?" he yelled back, knowing damn well the answer was no. "Do you have any idea how many hours it takes to run a business? Would you like me to go back to the bar and work 'till three or four in the morning six nights a week? Then I'd never see you, and I certainly wouldn't see Daisy. I'd be burned out from all the drunks, and I'd probably have lung cancer in a few more years!" He sat down on the stairs and lowered his voice. "There's nothing else I can do—who's going to hire a guy my age who only made it to grade eleven? You knew what I was doing when you met me, and you're just going to have to deal with it. I love growing pot; I love everything about it. It's the best job I've ever had; and, you have to admit, the lifestyle is incredible. I'm not going to quit now; we have a child to look after, and we have to pay for this house. Do you want to give it all up and move back to the rental house in town?"

"No." I replied quietly, after trying my hardest not to answer him at all. How could I argue?

We had no idea just how much room the multitude of clones would require. Every room in the basement was filled to capacity, with plants spilling outside and stacked in the stairway. The basement flooded repeatedly, and trackers with grow lights constantly hummed back and forth over the sea of green. Michael worked alone, putting in as many as eighteen hours a day, stopping only to eat or replenish his growing supplies. He looked forward to Tony's help and company, come planting time.

* * *

MAY 15—*Tony arrived today with one small suitcase and a big bag filled with cookies, chocolate bars and various other unhealthy, sugared treats. He's by far the shyest person I've ever met but seems like a really nice kid.*

"How's it going, Tony?" I asked cheerfully.

"Fine," came the barely audible reply.

"How was your drive up?"

"Fine."

"Come on in. Can we get you anything?"

"No, I'm fine."

"And how's your mom? Is everything okay with Don and April?"

"Fine."

"Well, make yourself at home."

With hunched shoulders and a New York Yankees baseball cap all but obscuring his face, Tony slowly made his way into the living room and curled up on the couch.

It was a touchy thing, hiring an old friend's child; but this kid looked downright freakish. Tony was a sweet but uncommonly shy nineteen-year-old whose good looks belied a personality so introverted he often had trouble with simple conversations. He was six-foot-two, with his mother's thin, muscular build and the same long, thick hair, though his was black rather than blond. Girls constantly noticed him, but Tony was petrified of human contact; and, while most teenagers were socializing and testing boundaries, Tony was happiest alone at his computer or sitting on a couch somewhere reading a small-appliance manual. He had never smoked pot, taken a drink of alcohol, had a date or held down a job. He was also the self-professed laziest person alive. Tony had refused to work at all during high school, which had led to endless testing and counseling. The tests revealed a way-above-average IQ and an incredibly stubborn attitude.

Although he had known Michael almost all his life and had grown up thinking of him as an uncle, Tony's attitudes made the transition to paid employee difficult. He literally would not speak unless spoken to; and when he did talk it was so quietly that his curt, one-word answers usually went unheard. On the job, he only did what was asked of him and nothing more. At the end of the day he returned to the couch and curled up into the fetal position, eventually forming a small dent on one side of the old brown sofa.

Around the house, with just Daisy and I, it was different. I spent most of my days alone with Daisy and welcomed the company of anyone who could say more than *goo-goo* or *da-da*. I enjoyed Tony and developed a close relationship with him. He was gentle and quiet and clean, and our baby was totally in love with him. Daisy's first word was "Toey."

* * *

> MAY 26—*Ronnie was over again. I can't figure out why Michael hangs on to these losers from his past; and this secluded home is a curse when it comes to company, a magnet for lost souls. Most people get out here and end up staying for a week; but if Ronnie ever so much as thinks about staying the night, Michael can find himself a new family. This guy gives me the creeps.*

He always arrived unannounced, barged through the front door and yelled "Hey, Hokenson, you got any pot?" on his way down the stairs to help himself, no matter what the answer. I gave him anything he wanted just to get rid of him and would then spend the next few minutes following the trail of cigarette butts, beer cans and dog shit left by him and his constant companion, Riley.

Michael felt sorry for Ronnie and assured me he was once considered a "god." He called himself Ronnie Love, the Love Machine, though any love felt for or by Ronnie is a thing of the past. But Michael remembered the old days—like the time when he and Ronnie were sitting on a stone wall outside a night club and the Love Machine embarrassed a cop...

* * *

Michael sat backwards on the wall, facing a park; and Ronnie stood beside him, smoking a cigarette. The two young friends had come outside for fresh air; they were talking about a girl Ronnie had just met and what a shame it was that she had a boyfriend. Suddenly,

46

Ronnie dashed across the street and stopped in front of a bank—a tall, imposing building of solid brick with bars covering the windows. The Love Machine then drew a match from his pocket, lit it and jumped up to place it on a windowsill high above the street.

Of course, the match fizzled out in seconds, making it necessary for Ronnie to light another and leap up to the window once again. Michael watched from across the street, laughing uncontrollably as Ronnie lit match after match, in a mock attempt to set the building on fire.

A policeman watched from inside his shiny new cruiser one street away. He recognized the troublemaking pair, turned on his siren and gunned the engine, approaching the men from the wrong direction on a one-way street.

The officer screeched to a stop beside Ronnie, wound down his window and yelled angrily, "Hey, what the fuck do you think you're you doing?"

The government had recently issued smaller, more fuel-efficient highway cars to replace the powerful giants of the sixties and seventies. Ronnie had his back to the street, his eyes still focused on the bank. He turned around slowly, grinning, and in a childlike voice quipped, "My, my, my. It's a little baby police car."

After seconds of uncomfortable silence, "Fuck you!" yelled the humiliated cop as he continued up the street—in the wrong direction—in the tiny new car.

* * *

Michael simply preferred to remember Ronnie as he had been in the past. Now almost forty, he had huge black circles under his eyes, a chipped front tooth and yellowish-brown skin from an overloaded liver. But Ronnie still acted Svengali-like and treated me like a whore.

"Hey, wench, bend over and get the Love Machine a cold beer will you?"

And I put up with the guy because I knew the alternative was arguing with my husband, and pot seemed to supply us with a steady stream of material for arguments as it was.

* * *

JUNE 1—*Michael is experimenting again and getting really carried away in the basement. We fought all morning over where and how our money was disappearing and how the flooding of the basement has got to stop. I spent four hours cleaning up ice-cold water full of ruined collectables and dirt while Daisy wailed at the top of her lungs, trapped in her baby swing. Today, I hate the pot world.*

Besides collecting junk and telling tall tales, Michael has always been famous for experimenting. For his third year, he decided to try organic topsoil to save money and reduce the risk of exposure to himself as a grower. A problem all large-scale growers have is the acquisition of literally tons of supplies. Police often watch hydroponics stores, and anyone can spot a pot grower at the local farm and garden shop as he buys eighty-five bales of sterile dirt and several hundred pounds of fertilizers.

This year, Michael avoided the problem by hiring dump trucks to deliver loads of black peat to our secluded home. Purported to be nutrient rich, the black gold—as it was called—was designed to grow high-yielding plants with very little use of chemical fertilizer. Michael saved a bundle and was thrilled with the prospect of growing cheaply and organically.

Another experiment that year was the Indian Reserve patch. It was a large-scale gamble, but Michael considered himself an authority on Indians because he had lots of Native friends. He assured me the police would never fly over reserve land looking for pot. This gave him the freedom to grow massive rows of pot instead of well-spaced solitary plants hidden from view. He hired a local pothead and single mother of three named Carmella to help him and Tony pack the soil through the bush in five-gallon buckets and garbage bags.

* * *

JUNE 10—*Today I was part of the crew. Carmella was over an hour late at our meeting place. I think Michael has discovered another winner.*

She sheepishly approached the truck in a rumpled, stained T-shirt that read *M-U-I-P-O, Support Poppy Day,* the faded remains of bright red poppies straining across her spongy breasts. She started babbling some long-winded explanation; but Michael waved his hand impatiently, not interested in the excuse and anxious to get to work.

By nine-thirty, the air was gathering heat from the sun's rays as we all piled into the big blue work truck. Sweat ran down my face and formed a puddle above my lip as I sat squished between Carmella and Michael. Carmella talked nonstop the entire trip, a home-rolled cigarette jumping up and down in the corner of her mouth. Tony sat quietly against the door, arms folded, head down, eyes squinted shut.

Finally, we reached the reservation. I felt close to vomiting—the smell of Carmella's body odor mingled with cigarette smoke and sweat was overpowering.

Six feet tall, fifty pounds overweight and always going on about something, Carmella worked like a dog once she got going. Her massive body was strong as well as fat; and, despite her sweating and groaning, she was amazing in the bush. Tony trudged determinedly through the dense growth in her wake and Michael and I followed.

We dug trenches, lined them with soaker hoses and filled them with topsoil. There was no water in this particular area, which Michael considered another plus for growing—no one would think to look for marijuana on a dry piece of reserve land. Big Blue packed two hundred-fifty gallons of water at a time, and a converted Caterpillar battery powered a pump in the back of the truck. Once a week, Michael and Tony sneaked through the overgrown forest and delivered water and food to the trenches through hoses attached to the pump. The crop thrived.

I really wanted to get back in shape after having our baby. I had developed an unsightly gut and flabby, post-baby legs; and I figured the answer was outdoor marijuana cultivation. While Michael conducted his experiments, I readied myself for my first solo patch. I had the perfect growing area right behind our house, a southern exposure on a steep hillside.

Marijuana loves uninterrupted sunlight, and a slope provides protection from frost in the fall. I borrowed Tony to help get dirt up the hill and into the patch. I wasn't strong enough to dig Cousin Jimmy-size holes, so I used large fiber pots Michael had acquired for an experiment but wasn't using. I had no idea as I planted this first patch that pot loves being grown above ground in containers. The heat from the sun is retained, and the confined space causes the plants to become root-bound. This enables them to bud quicker, and the pot can be harvested early. I had some beginner's luck myself.

The view from my secret garden was spectacular. The huge, pristine lake below was panoramic. I could see endless stretches of sky and water, yet I was completely hidden from the world. Every two or three days, I would strap on my baby monitor and run up the hill while little Daisy slept peacefully in her crib. The length of her mid-morning nap was more than I needed to tend to my garden, and no aerobics class could equal the cardiovascular workout I was getting.

We had water line buried a few inches underground running from our garage to partway up the hill. An electric pump helped the water reach its destination, which was just to the edge of my patch. There, I mixed five-gallon pails of fertilizer and hauled them straight up and across to eighty-five plants. Each pail would do three to five plants until they got big and demanding, then each bucket was only good for one or two. As the plants became large, I became strong and looked forward to each workout.

My schedule that summer rarely varied. I spent the majority of my days alone with Daisy, which I loved. I made most of her baby food and used cloth diapers, which required me to be at home a lot. Most days we walked a few miles with the stroller and spent every waking hour together. I only went to a town if we needed something. If we had company, I was consumed by a cycle of cooking, cleaning, serving and more cleaning. In between, Daisy and I would escape to the large upstairs bedroom and hide out together, undetected.

* * *

> JULY 21—*6:00 A.M. There is no relief from the heat. I've been forced to tend to my garden before the men leave for work. I just returned from watering, and the size of my plants has started to worry me. The record-breaking temperatures that have consumed most of June and July are making my plants grow like crazy. Two people died from heat stroke yesterday, and everyone is drained and edgy. But my garden is thriving—tall, thick and vibrant. The plants look like octopuses extending their long green tendrils in every direction, beckoning me to climb up the hill and feed them. Although it's a satisfying sight, I am beginning to experience paranoia. I can't imagine how they might look in another few months.*

I woke Michael and consulted him; he had a solution for my problem. He had read in one of his many new marijuana manuals that tying plants down increases yield and makes them less visible to unwanted eyes. So, we hiked up to the patch together to tie them all to the ground. This was an experiment that Michael had been yearning to try.

Most of the branches I attempted to tie I instead snapped. I was hot and impatient and hated that the sticky branches smeared resin all over me. Michael spotted me grumbling and fussing, lying on my stomach surrounded by broken branches and black flies. He, on the other hand, was loving and gentle and did an incredible job of rearranging my plants. The end result was amazing. The plants required subsequent tying during the summer, but the job grew easier as we discovered better methods. The patch was now low and sprawling, which made it almost impossible to see from the air. It also made working in the patch a nightmare.

I'd be running like hell with a full bucket of water as my next one was filling. Crash, thud, slop! The tie-downs that now covered the ground, nicely hidden beneath burgeoning branches of bud, would inevitably trip me. They were like land mines waiting to cut off my legs at the ankles. As I fell, I would lose my precious bucket, which would end up rolling and bouncing downhill until something stopped it; and the bucket that was filling would overflow, its contents spilled onto the ground. This was part of the fun that growing pot had to offer. I'd return to the house covered in scratches, bruises, bug bites, dirt and sweat. At least, my gut was getting smaller.

Sometimes, I'd have a day where I felt strong and capable...until a horsefly would come after me. Carnivorous and relentless, the horsefly is my biggest fear. Just the sight of one would cause me to drop whatever I was carrying and run clumsily through the bush like the coward I truly was. Or the black flies and mosquitoes would encircle me like a plague, humming and buzzing until I felt close to insanity. I hated to share my garden with these insects and was ashamed that I let them get the better of me.

There aren't many days spent growing anything that Mother Nature doesn't remind you who's boss. You have no control over the weather, a critical element that can make or break any farmer's year. When the inevitable heat and bugs finally die down, there is always an equally unsavory replacement—a nice, crisp, early frost or a hungry deer or rabbit. Mold can appear late in the season and wipe out an entire crop in merely days. I didn't know it at the time, but I actually had it easy for my virgin crop.

* * *

JULY 31—*I can't believe it's our wedding day! Time has flown by, with the never-ending cycle of pot growing consuming us. The day has been smoldering from the moment we awoke, and our house is full of people. Everyone is asking me questions. I've got to be selfish today and let everyone fend for themselves—today is our day.*

I had become surprisingly nervous and, as my best friend suggested, attempted to calm myself with champagne. So much, in fact, that Michael literally had to hold me up and prompt me to speak during our poignant exchange of vows. (For this, Cousin Jimmy gave me two thumbs up.) Daisy screamed through the entire ceremony as all four of her grandparents stuffed her with food and fretted over her. I was grateful for this distraction—and so relieved when the formalities were over.

Blissful and married, Michael and I breathed a joint sigh of relief and were happy to get back to our secluded house and our respective gardens. I realized as I looked at the beautiful antique ring on my finger that I was wholly committed to Michael for the rest of my life. I was officially his partner in everything and had to be supportive and dedicated to our chosen life of crime.

The human presence in the wilderness is inevitably destructive, at the very least upsetting the delicate balance of the earth. When Michael returned to his main garden he fell to his knees, mouth agape. He studied the contorted patch before him, trying to figure out what had become of his crop. He crashed through the scorching forest, babbling aloud to the birds and chipmunks, begging for an answer as to what horrible deed they might have witnessed.

After hours of carefully examining each and every plant and playing several scenarios out in his mind, Michael realized that Jimmy and I had made the holes "hot." We had poured so much fertilizer into the soil the year before that anything planted in the chemical-laden earth would actually burn. We had recently read about this condition but were powerless to change the fact that all of last year's big, beautiful holes had been planted. Snow and rain had leached the ground to some degree but, in this case, couldn't compensate for our interference. Every healthy clone planted in the hot zone had immediately gone into bud.

This is not a marijuana grower's dream come true. The fertilizer forced the baby plants to skip vegetating—growing—and start producing little baby buds that signaled the end of their life cycle. We had over three hundred miniature, deformed plants that had been beautiful, healthy clones only weeks before.

After further reading and discussion with a seasoned grower, we learned that, for fifty dollars-worth of lime and a few hours work, we could have neutralized the soil in every hole. Lime restores pH and reduces acidity. But we didn't know any of that in the spring, and Jimmy and I were—rightly—held responsible for the multitude of undesirable midgets scattered across the property.

My garden was another story altogether. Other than my undignified aerobics, everything was going well for me my first year. Most of my plants were on their way to yielding well over half a pound each. The "black gold" soil was a total scam; my burning desire to overfeed my plants their only saving grace. I used fish fertilizer, foliar fertilizer, water-soluble fertilizer, slow-release fertilizer and any of Michael's supplies that I could sneak without him knowing. I pushed my girls to their limits like a coach guiding a winning team of athletes, dousing them all with steroids until their leaf tips started to burn. I was headed for a bumper crop.

This was the year I realized just how much it costs to grow any large-scale crop. If you aren't able to harvest at least some of each patch, it's easy to actually lose money. It's also difficult to budget throughout the year when payday comes only once, and when you need to consistently buy so many things: soil, fertilizer, gas, bear mace, bug spray, books, tools, cloning trays, rooting agents, peat pods, hoses, rabbit cages, tie-downs, stakes, camping equipment, truck, power saw, rifle, fungicides, pesticides, wolf urine, tarps, garbage bags, scales, spring wages, guard's wages, clipper's wages— the list goes on and on and on. Anything the plants need, you buy them, even though you know there's a very good chance some thief will come along and steal a hefty percentage of your hard work and investment in the fall. And there's an equal chance the police will find some of your areas. They are dedicated, assisted by many civilians and progressively better funded each year. Michael has always considered this part of doing business and adds a few extra plants for the drug squad and rip-offs.

The Labor Day weekend of '94, we gave generously to the RCMP. Every plant and every piece of equipment in every trench on the Indian Reserve disappeared two days before harvest. Not a leaf on the ground remained; and the earth surrounding each trench was smooth and flat, as if it had been raked and tamped back to its original state.

I was along to help harvest the day we went to bring in the first load of plants. Daisy was with her grandparents for the week, and I wanted to compare Michael's crop with mine. We had converted the basement of our new home to a clipping area, and we had a crew waiting for our return.

Michael had recently hired a new employee for the harvest season, and he'd arrived in time for the first cutting. This latest rookie was Willy, the stepson of Herman, the pot connoisseur who had helped us the season before. Willy was nineteen, longhaired and well on his way with drugs, booze, tattoos and girls. We couldn't possibly corrupt him, so he had moved in to take Tony's place.

Tony had been unceremoniously fired in late August when Michael felt close to a nervous breakdown. He wanted an energetic and hard-working employee, not a lazy kid who rarely spoke and would only do something when specifically directed. Actually, Michael said it was all those hours of uncomfortable silence that really drove him over the edge.

Tony's only true passion in life was computers, and I felt we were wrong in offering him a job he could never feel passionate about. Taking a city kid with uncallused hands and hay fever and plunging him into the bush with a crazy, pot-growing pseudo-uncle wasn't exactly a recipe for success. The day Tony was finally fired—after lying in the house, on the couch, in the fetal position, while Michael was outside, alone, for over an hour preparing for the day—he handed in his hours, figured to the minute. They included: August 27, 10:06 A.M.—fired. Tony went home to his mother's.

Michael, Willy and I set out to harvest the reserve patch. Michael had checked the plants on the previous Thursday, and he conservatively estimated the area at a hundred pounds. He decided not to haul pot on a long weekend because of the numerous roadblocks that were common in our tourist-engorged area. Monday evening, just as the sun dipped behind the purple hills, we came to the first trench. For a moment, I thought we were in the wrong spot. I could tell by Michael's face and the open mouth of an eager Willy that we were, in fact, exactly where we should be.

I felt as if I'd been punched in the stomach. The patch was gone. Not only had every plant disappeared but there wasn't a trace of the sprawling trench. The area had been returned to its original state, revealing nothing of our summer project. There was nothing to do but get back in the truck and drive through the thick forest until we reached the next trench.

It looked much like the first one, and the nauseous feeling continued to overwhelm me. Michael started laughing as I became increasingly angry and confused. I saw no humor in the situation, only wasted time and money. Michael continued to giggle until I wanted to slap him. He always took tragedy far better than I. Willy, like me, was devastated.

"Shit, man. This is sick, Mickey. Goddamn. Do you have much other shit out there, man? Just fucking sick. Cops…fucking pricks!"

We salvaged only a good-quality pruning tool left behind by the police, which we took for a souvenir. The entire area had been wiped out and combed clean. Two area newspapers mentioned the police's find within days. Back home in the empty makeshift clipping room, morale was low.

We still had some patches to harvest but not enough to support a large crew. All the cleaners were sent home with the exception of one. He had been recommended by a long-time friend and was totally committed to the project. He had taken a thirty-day leave of absence from his job and traveled all the way from Whistler just to help us out.

His name was James Foreman the Second, an ex-Olympic diver and extreme skier as well as a part-time alcoholic. James was handsome and distinguished-looking, with short graying hair and a thick white moustache, giving him the appearance of a man somewhat older than his thirty-nine years. When James liked something, he loved it. He liked Jimmy Buffet, which meant that all the music in his collection was performed by Jimmy Buffet. He had listened to the same songs for the last twenty years, updating records and eight-tracks to cassettes and, eventually, owning the complete collection on CD.

James also liked smoking pot, drinking beer and wearing clothes by Ralph Lauren. And he could do all of his favorite things while clipping his favorite plant and be very well paid for his efforts. Although an inexperienced clipper, James was eager and excited.

James loved to spend money and party but had the discipline to work sixteen-hour days by himself. Every day Michael brought him a huge load of pot and arranged it in buckets of water in the cold room. By the end of his first week with us, James dubbed himself "The Vidal Sassoon of Clipping." He single-handedly cleaned over sixty pounds of pot in less than a month, which is impressive, and was fairly low-maintenance as a houseguest. James required one weekly shower and one Polo outfit to work in; he drank only beer and coffee and subsisted on one meal a day. Single and good-natured, he was clearly the perfect employee.

About ten days after James's arrival, some of my plants were ready to be harvested. My dear friend Sherry returned and was joined by an eternally late, perpetually stoned Carmella. Michael had been impressed with Carmella's work filling the trenches on the Indian Reserve, and she told him she had previous experience clipping. We hired her and Sherry to work part-time and relieve James on his occasional days off.

Every day, Michael would go out to one of his various areas and return with a load of fresh pot. I only joined him a couple of times—the reserve bust had taken the wind out of my sails. My secret garden was safe and harvestable, and I couldn't visit it enough. It was so exciting to sprint up the hill with snippers and empty garbage bags and carefully walk down under a heavy load of fragrant branches. Every time I chose the ripest plants, I first had to complete my ritual of squishing and smelling every bud I could reach. Michael and I were both obsessive-compulsive with this behavior, which was totally unnecessary. We just loved marijuana and how it felt and smelled and looked. I also loved the fact that my patch generated just under $100,000. I was hooked, no longer just a grower's wife. This was the beginning of my new career.

We'd lost another two areas to thieves, and I asked to be spared all the details. There were second cuttings waiting to be harvested in several patches, and it seemed as if the year would never end. By this point, I wanted it to all be over. I wanted my house back, the guests gone, the smell gone, the endless phone calls to stop. I secretly prayed for snow. The crew was mentally and physically exhausted, and fuses were beginning to shorten. But it's never over until the last plant is clipped and dried; only then can you have your life back— until next year.

Michael had quite a number of *indica* plants in '94, lengthening an already long and nerve-wracking harvest. There are three types of marijuana: *sativa, indica* and *ruderellis*. Most North American growers stick to *sativa* strains, which mature fairly early. *Indica* are short, stocky and very potent; but they require a longer growing season. *Ruderellis* strains are hard to acquire, possibly because they are low-yielding and undesirable.

The first of the trial *indicas* were ready in early November, and they were well worth the wait. The plants were beautiful—deep purple, fragrant and they produced some of the best pot Michael had ever grown from a technical standpoint. Unfortunately, the strain had come from a friend who was unable to get it again, and so it was gone but never forgotten. This started an ongoing experiment in regenerating mother plants from nothing but a bottom stalk.

It was almost Christmas by the time we completed the last transaction. Our buyer still wanted more pot, so Michael introduced him to a new friend of ours who'd had trouble selling all his product. The meeting was very successful: forty-five pounds of primo pot exchanged hands, and our buyer made five hundred dollars per pound by simply buying for one price and reselling the next day with his fee added on. As a token of his appreciation, he gave Michael a big bag of cocaine.

Michael's past had been full of cocaine—he'd sold it, snorted a ton of it, over-dosed on it and, subsequently, given it up. Not to look a gift horse in the mouth, he accepted the evil white powder and gave it to me to hide. We had no idea what to do with the stuff but knew it was worth a few dollars. I was wholly in charge of turning it into money or trading it for something useful. I put it in a crock-pot on the kitchen counter and we both forgot about it.

Year Four, 1995

Getting in Deeper

JANUARY 3—*I had the dream again. A huge black helicopter is suddenly hovering over our house. There is no warning, no noise—it just appears from the north, flattening the treetops inches away from the roof. I creep to the window and see the foreboding bird. It is full of policemen and DEA agents dressed in SWAT uniforms, gas masks obscuring their faces. One man is hanging out the side door with a rifle pointed right at me. There is no escape. Our house is full of marijuana, and they've finally caught us. The chopper is deafening by now, and I run downstairs to the basement to get away from the noise. I panic; I can't think what to do, what to grab, where to run...and then I awaken, drenched in sweat, my heart pounding.*

This is my recurring nightmare; I have it every couple of months. I inch closer to Michael and curl up on his chest, removing my T-shirt to wipe the back of my neck. I tell him about the dream, and he hugs me and assures me that everything is okay. Growing pot is not a crime worthy of a SWAT team. And we're Canadian—there is no DEA and no shiny black helicopter patrolling our neighborhood. We grow pot largely because the punishment in B.C. is minimal; the rewards far outweigh the risks. We will never be shot at or sent to prison. I realize he is completely right and try to fall back to sleep. But the dream upsets me, and I can't shake it off for a couple of days.

Michael and I decided to go on a holiday. We both needed a break from our crazy life and the numbing temperatures sweeping across the country. We had always wanted to see Belize and the Mayan ruins that dot Central America, so choosing a destination was easy. My only problem was that I'd never been away from Daisy for more than a few days, and even that was usually difficult for me.

Fretting and anxious, I packed Daisy's crib, her playpen, toys, clothes, food, etc. So much stuff, in fact, that I started crying at the sight of her empty bedroom. My heart was breaking, and we hadn't even left the house.

I knew I needed to toughen up a bit. I pulled myself up off the floor of the cheerful pink room, wiped my running eyes and nose and scooped little Daisy into my arms and took her to my parents' farm. Michael had a lot of preparations to make before the trip as he hastily finished converting the garage to a grow room. He wanted the new room up and running before our departure, which was only days away; and he needed me there to help him.

Things weren't going well for Michael in the new room, and he worked almost nonstop for two days. The night before we were due to leave I went out to check on him and take him dinner; and when I opened the door and asked how things were going, I thought he looked kind of odd. He was sitting on an overturned bucket staring blankly at the floor. His skin was pale, and he was shaking. Timidly, I asked what was wrong; and he explained, with difficulty, that he'd given himself a mild electrical shock a while earlier. He had no idea how long he'd been sitting there.

This is every grower and grower's wife's nightmare. It's worse than being arrested, jailed, ripped off, mauled or injured in the bush: finding your husband dead in the garage amidst an illegal grow operation. But Michael wasn't dead; he'd been lucky—again. He was just stunned; and, a short time later, he went back to work and completed the project on schedule.

The sad thing about this near-tragedy was that we didn't need the money. A realtor friend of Michael's had talked him into operating the room as partners; the risk was all ours, but it was an opportunity for the eternal experimenter to learn the craft of hydroponics.

Jimmy and Michael were still close, though no longer partners; and it was really Jimmy who needed the money. He had grown without the help of Michael—on the land they owned together and had agreed not to grow on—and had boozed the summer away, neglecting his plants. He'd also put patches in really stupid areas, and thieves had worked him over pretty hard. Michael had promised Jimmy the proceeds of his share of the new room; all Jimmy had to do was check on things while we were away. Jimmy should never have quit his straight job, but at least he was attempting to gain some knowledge of horticulture.

We did go to Belize and had a wonderful holiday. I came home alone, after only one week, because I missed Daisy terribly. Michael had fun by himself but was on a tight budget because I'd lost most of our money on the plane.

A problem with large amounts of undeclared cash lying around is simply what to do with it at times. We'd just sold a few stray pounds on our way to catch our plane in Vancouver, so we had a surplus of twenty-dollar bills. I exchanged them into American money at the airport.

Upon our arrival in Belize, I left my purse on the plane accidentally for a couple of minutes as I sleepily walked across the hot tarmac to the entrance of the tiny airport. I realized what I'd done and quickly ran back up the stairs and into the nearly empty plane. One of the stewards looked extremely nervous as he assured me there was no purse left behind. He stood directly in front of me, blocking the aisle and fidgeting.

Finally, a female employee said, "For God's sake, let the girl go and look for her purse. How is she going to start a holiday without it?"

The steward relented and moved. I rushed back to my seat; and there was my purse, sitting right where I'd left it. I never thought to look in my wallet, and it wouldn't have helped anyway—twenty-nine hundred untraceable American dollars had vanished in less than five minutes. I still had a few traveler's checks, but the loss of the cash seriously put a damper on our trip. Michael and I had to suck it up and realize this was part of the game—easy come, easy go.

We had so much money at that time we were careless, and it didn't really matter. We gave handfuls of money to strangers and friends alike if we thought they needed it. I stuffed money into drawers, boxes of cereal, closets, vases and shoes—anywhere. Often, I'd forget where I'd put it and then be pleasantly surprised later. A lot of the people we know live like this.

The community we live in subsists mainly on income related to marijuana. The area I speak of is bigger than Vancouver, yet it has no high school. There are professional clippers, clone makers, growers, middlemen and laborers. Every second home contains a pot grower, people you would never in a million years suspect—the very old, the very young, loggers, farmers, PTA members, realtors, plumbers, electricians, equipment operators, mechanics, truck drivers, waitresses and many people with their own small businesses who just can't survive financially without augmenting their income.

Most of this money goes directly back into the community. We provide jobs, buy groceries, hardware, clothes, gardening supplies, vehicles, gas, etc. Most smart pot growers also file income tax every year or two and pay their share of taxes. Without this illicit income, our whole community and hundreds of others like it would probably collapse. The social welfare system would take many families over because, of course, there are no jobs for us all. It's realizing things like this that enables people to keep growing.

As we see it, our embarrassing, blatantly corrupt government doesn't exactly encourage intelligent people to play by the rules. After the multi-billion-dollar ferry scandal in B.C and conflicts of interest with so many premiers, I had completely given up on the system and vowed to do whatever I wanted, my conscience allowing. It's legal to sit in your living room and smoke cancer-causing cigarettes or drink alcohol until you throw up, but it's illegal to smoke the flowers of an herb that's been grown and used for thousands of years. I just can't agree with a law like that.

Besides, there's no incentive for people like us to stop growing pot. We believe alcohol and cigarettes to be among the most evil and destructive drugs on the planet, and statistics prove beyond any doubt they are big takers of lives; yet their use and abuse remains rampant as the government cashes in. And both of these potentially fatal substances are legal—what brilliant minds decided that for us? There is still no evidence of this sort against marijuana.

Now, of course, medical marijuana is okay, as long as the government decides for you whether you need it or not. If you have cancer it's legal, if you have glaucoma it's legal, if you have AIDS it's legal. What if you just want to unwind after a rough day at the office and enjoy a smoke like you could a nice glass of chardonnay? The absurdity of laws like this encourages people to rebel.

We spent our next few months off elaborately planning to continue our lives as criminals. The rest of that winter was relatively uneventful. Tony returned to our area after spending a few months back home with his mother; he was finally ready to live on his own. Still painfully quiet and socially challenged, Tony expressed a desire to learn how to grow pot indoors. If anyone needed to embark on a career path offering a steady paycheck with minimal contact with the public, it was Tony. So, we agreed to provide him with help and knowledge. I was glad that he was living only a few miles away, and that he and Michael were over their failed employer/employee relationship.

Meantime, Daisy reminded me that I had an unfinished project to complete. One morning, I fed her breakfast and put her in her playpen so I could clean the kitchen. She pulled herself to the counter and started reaching for things to investigate. I immediately moved the crockpot away from her because it was heavy and had sharp edges. I took the lid off for some reason, and there was the stashed cocaine. I stared at it for a while with no idea what to do and finally phoned Carmella. I really didn't know many people in the area, and Carmella kind of knew everyone. I prayed she could turn the dope into money, once and for all.

Although she was currently a pot smoker and nothing more, Carmella's past had included cocaine. She pulled back her matted mane of hair, rolled up a scrap of paper to use as a conduit and tested it. She pronounced it very high quality, every inch of her bulk suddenly invigorated.

It was a strange scene—two housewives pondering the fate of a quarter-pound of cocaine over coffee and bran muffins at ten o'clock in the morning. Carmella took a sample and put it in her purse next to a mushy pack of Twinkies. She said there was only one person she could think of who possibly might want to buy some, and he had money and lived nearby. I told her to take whatever she needed and go for it.

A few hours later, she came back and announced that she had a sale. His name was Rob Hudson, and he wanted to buy an ounce. Apparently, Rob and his wife were about to host a Grey Cup party.

I drove to the would-be buyer's house with mixed emotions. I so badly wanted to get rid of the powdery white clump of contraband that gave me the creeps. Realistically, the easiest thing to do would be to dump it in the bush or flush it down the toilet, like they do in the movies. On the other hand, I was only human and just as greedy as the next guy. I saw no reason not to profit from the sale of this crap if someone wanted to buy it. By this time, I had come so far from the law-abiding nurse and "normal" citizen that I used to be I was almost a different person.

As we pulled into the yard, I was slightly shocked as I realized that Rob and his wife were local business people and PTA members— the last people I would expect to be buying cocaine. Was there anyone in this backwoods community who wasn't involved with drugs? Even wholesome, organic Carmella could find a market for a large amount of coke in less than four hours.

Carmella went in first and gave the people time to usher their children into the living room. Then I was called into the house, which was actually two trailers joined together by a creative drywall specialist. Rob and his tiny blond wife took me into their makeshift office and paid me in full. Immediately, they started chopping up cocaine and snorting it. Rob was over six-feet-six, and it looked to me like there might not be a whole lot of dope left for the Grey Cup party at this rate. Even Carmella was partaking. I stayed only long enough to get paid and exchange phone numbers and quickly made my exit.

Tony had come along for the ride to give me moral support

because Michael had said he wanted nothing to do with it. We drove home, satisfied, with $1300. We hurried into the living room; and I eagerly reported the details of my meeting to Michael, who sat calmly on the couch smiling. He shared my surprise over who had just bought what we considered to be an unhealthy amount of cocaine. The Hudsons were well-respected members of the community, both of them highly involved in local school and business functions.

Two days later, Rob called and asked if I could drive over for another visit. Greedy and willing, we weighed out another ounce, and off I went with Tony.

This time, things did not go as planned. When I arrived, Rob called me into his bedroom; and, like a lamb to the slaughter, I went. I gave him a bag containing what I thought he wanted—another ounce. For this, Rob gave me a crumpled up hundred-dollar bill, a substantial amount shy of the mark. But he already had the package open, and he was a lot bigger than me. I really wanted to get the hell out of his ugly bedroom. I listened to his excuses about the bank machine not giving him enough money as he towered over me, suddenly permeating my personal space and making me uncomfortable. Breathlessly, I told him he could pay me later.

When I got back in my car, Tony said, "Oh, my God. You just fronted a total stranger fifteen hundred dollars-worth of cocaine. I think we're in shit. What is Michael going to say?"

But Michael was great. He said there was no need to worry at this point—the guy had a wife and kids and a job in the community. We decided to give Rob a few days to make good on his debt; and, slowly but surely, he did. As a matter of fact, ounce by ounce, gram by gram, Rob eventually bought every bit of cocaine we had.

In the end, we just gave the last of it to him to get rid of it. I thought he must have had a lot of big friends like himself, and that Grey Cup must be a long sporting event. I had no idea as I supplied him with cocaine that he was smoking it all with his wife. There had never been a Grey Cup party or any other party involving people other than Rob and the missus. Other than his appetite for drugs, Rob seemed like a pretty nice guy.

None of this mattered to me to me now nor would I have cared if I had known it at the time. If an adult wants to put something into his or her body, be it a greasy meal at McDonald's or hundreds of cigarettes—or chocolate-covered grasshoppers, for that matter—it's none of my business or anyone else's, the way I see it. This was part of my problem with drug laws in general. How could it ever be anyone's right to dictate what other people put in their bodies? We should all be free to decide what to eat and drink and smoke.

I don't believe in fast food or candy or prescription drugs for every little ailment, but our whole society thrives on people's ability to make these choices. I was sad that the Hudsons obviously had a drug problem, but it was their problem to deal with. At least Rob got the kids to hockey on time and, ultimately, had the will power to go to detox.

With the cocaine project over and spring just around the corner, it was time to start cutting clones. Again. By this time, Michael had two indoor hydroponic rooms—one each in our house and garage. He just couldn't get the yield he wanted out of the rooms, so he was forced to continue experimenting. This meant a constant supply of clones was necessary year-round. The large reservoirs used in hydroponics coupled with Michael's forgetful nature ensured a weekly basement flooding. The worst problem in both rooms, however, was a spider mite infestation.

Spider mites are prolific, destructive little bastards that love marijuana rooms. The warm temperature and high humidity associated with indoor gardening are the perfect environment for these insects. When a spider mite population reaches colony size, the bugs spin webs from plant to plant and can easily cover every square inch of the crop. The plants turn yellow and crispy as the life is literally sucked out of them by the millions of hungry mites. One femme fatale is capable of producing thirteen million babies in just one month.

Doing battle with spider mites is a job fit for a warrior. The mites usually prevail over the human and become immune to whatever pesticide they are doused with. Michael fought valiantly but eventually surrendered. The system he'd run for over a year was dismantled and abandoned. The plants had been over seven feet tall, the product of several months of growth. As the plants grew, so did the initially invisible colony of death. Michael vowed that the next system would involve a significantly shorter growing time and much smaller plants.

Tony came to harvest the final crispy, yellow crop with me while Michael watched Daisy. We sat on the concrete floor of the garage among the webs and humming ballasts to clip what looked like an ounce or two of poor-quality pot. I was wary of the fact that our friendly neighborhood bear had just been spotted, so we clipped in silence. Her cub had been recently snooping around in the other part of the garage and she often used our balcony as a walkway. Tony, whose bachelor menu consisted of cookies, frozen cakes that contained shellac and Coke, begged to bring a box of cookies into our clipping room. I disapproved and said no; but the cookies came anyway, and an hour or two into our messy, pathetic clip I heard a commotion on the sundeck.

We both assumed it was Michael emptying buckets off the balcony, a common occurrence year-round. Minutes later, a long black nose poked open the door; and there, standing over us sniffing the air, was the bear. From where we were sitting on the floor, she looked huge. I jumped up and scrambled over Tony, spilling the remnants of the forbidden cookies all over the floor. The plants had been hung on a makeshift clothesline; and the sticky, mite-infested pot attached itself to my hair and sweatshirt as I hurtled towards the door to the house. The poor bear must have been equally surprised because she spun around and fled for the forest with speed that I wouldn't have believed possible.

The noise on the sundeck had been the bear throwing all my potted plants over the edge after ripping them from their containers. Shaken and humbled, Tony and I returned to the garage and cautiously clipped the remaining plants. Michael dismantled the grow room and hauled the equipment to his acreage.

* * *

MARCH 8—*Everywhere we go, everyone we talk to, it's pot, pot, pot. Why is this stuff so all-consuming, the topic of every conversation? It's just not that exciting. Bigger buds, better areas, who got ripped off, who did well, who lost everything, who's growing indoors, WHO CARES! When I was a nurse I didn't only talk of changing dressings and how to best drain a urine bag. I don't know why we can't just grow this shit like the rest of our plants and be done with it. And everyone we know here is a pot grower or they want to become a pot grower. We're hardly allowed to talk to non-growers for fear of exposing ourselves. Sometimes, I wish they'd just come and arrest us and get it over with. Then, maybe we could try something new. Thank God, I have Daisy.*

As the gray days of winter lengthened into a welcome spring, we were blessed with a neighbor. His name was Kenny; he was an old friend of Michael's from the hotel and cocaine business. Just down the road from us was an empty rental house, frequently used by pot growers. Somehow, Kenny got wind of its availability and was only too happy to take it.

Cocaine had all but ruined Kenny's life, and he was determined to leave the city and straighten himself out. He had no driver's license, no money and almost no contact with the rest of the world. He moved into his new home with an old German shepherd and two mangy cats from the SPCA. He literally couldn't go out and get into trouble.

Daisy had many aunts and very few uncles so Kenny became "Aunty Kenny." The couple of times during his hibernation that he actually did get out for a few hours, he had several local women fighting over him. Aunty Kenny was essentially a chick magnet. He had long, 80's hair and wore chains around his rubber boots. He was open and friendly with a crazy sense of humor. Kenny was one of those guys who always made lewd, goofy sexual come-ons but was funny and somehow not offensive. I guess the girls in our neighborhood found his style irresistible—to the point where he eventually had to change his phone number and stay clear of the local watering hole.

Kenny immediately turned his entire basement into a grow room, embarking on a journey of growth and learning. He fell in love with his indoor garden and enjoyed his pets and close proximity to nature. He eagerly anticipated his first outdoor crop and welcomed the hard work and long hours as a perfect distraction.

Michael wanted to expand my plantation behind our house because of its obvious success the first year. I adamantly said no. Aunty Kenny was putting in a patch just behind his house, and we'd share a common boundary. I also had this superstitious feeling that greed was the downfall of all growers. We argued back and forth, and finally I won and retained the right to use the patch just as it was.

Michael had made more money his second year with three hundred-eighty plants than he had with the whole rest of his crop of '94. Out of one thousand plants, thieves and police had reduced the harvestable number to around four hundred. With large distances between the areas, the plants didn't receive the daily TLC that the smaller crop had. This was the beginning of an ongoing disagreement between husband and wife on how much pot to grow every year. I always wanted to do less, Michael always wanted more.

One thing we agreed on was that it would be fun to put in a small crop at my parents' farm. My dad had just retired and was becoming restless and bored. He was fascinated with marijuana and eager to learn how to grow it. He had worked so hard all his life that he'd never had time to develop a hobby. His idea of a good time usually involved the outdoors and work as a form of leisure. He had no real experience growing anything, as my mother had always been in charge of their numerous gardens. On May 15th, Michael drove to the family farm with a power auger and dug one hundred-fifteen big, deep holes for his new father-in-law.

The best thing about my dad has always been his intelligence and open mind; he doesn't judge others for how they live or what they believe in. My parents both welcomed Michael into the family, dope grower or not. Neither of my parents drinks, and they've always thought of alcohol as the most disgusting and destructive drug of the century. Furthermore, from a gardener's standpoint, making a plant illegal is completely absurd. Opium poppies, tobacco and marijuana are all incredible plants that have been put into the same taboo category by government officials. For law-abiding, tax-paying citizens to agree with archaic and ridiculous laws like our marijuana laws is asking too much.

My mother never said much about Dad's summer project as she watched her husband become mesmerized with his new hobby. He worried a bit about the police at first but soon became pro-legalization. The fact that what he was growing was illegal was an unfortunate technicality that only made it worth more money.

My father came to Canada from Ireland in the late 1940s at the age of eighteen. He'd worked hard as a miner and, eventually, a diamond driller for more than forty years to be able to own his farm. Both of my parents had made sacrifices along the way and felt that he was entitled to grow whatever he liked on his land. And my mother grew tobacco and opium poppies every year.

Dad's patch was located in a small clearing about half a mile from the house. The spring that provided water for the large acreage flowed down the mountain and into a ten thousand-gallon reservoir. The overflow from the reservoir provided more than an adequate supply of water and was just a stone's-throw from the patch.

A great horned owl chose one of the tall birch trees near the new garden as her nesting place. Here she raised two babies, and it became an evening ritual for my parents to walk to the clearing with binoculars and watch the magnificent bird hunt for her owlets, soaring over the radiant marijuana plants. They also watched the bright green fan leaves reach towards the sky, gaining size and strength until they eventually gave way to tiny clumps of flowers.

With privacy, plenty of water and lots of support from Michael and me, Dad faced few problems as a pot grower. We provided him with a hundred-fifty healthy clones of a proven strain and the necessary help and directions to grow them.

My parents' farm is a donkey sanctuary; and the mischievous donkeys chewed several large, lovely plants immediately. Dad quickly built a corral around his garden, but the persistent animals continued to feed through the fence. Every few days, the donkeys would return to the patch and knock out a rail or two or find the smallest opening to squeeze a long neck through. Eventually, the outermost plants in the perimeter of the patch were sacrificed. I think Dad actually found this amusing; he could have locked the donkeys out of the area any time he wanted. Keeping the plants and animals harmonious was a humorous, ongoing challenge.

About twice a week, Michael or I would drive over and give the novice gardener supplies and directions. Completely unlike his daughter, Dad had a tendency to go light on the fertilizer. He filled his holes with garden compost and donkey manure and his maiden crop prospered. Soon, it was impossible to tell that the donkeys had thinned the patch. The clearing was loaded with tall, bushy plants as good as any we'd ever grown. By the end of that summer, Dad had purchased a hemp hat that sported a green, embroidered marijuana leaf. He was completely in awe of the plants he was growing.

When the first tiny white hairs appeared and buds began to form he was like a little kid waiting for Santa. He became obsessed with bud production and started to drive us crazy with descriptive daily phone calls. We begged him not to talk about buds and readiness and clipping and pot on the telephone, but he couldn't stop himself. Santa was on his way down the chimney, and Dad planned on being there with milk and cookies.

My secret garden was also doing well, but the yield was going to be down from the previous year. I was growing two different strains, which made it harder to maintain the plants. One strain was nearly finished while the other was only showing the early beginnings of buds. The weather was less than ideal, with colder temperatures and too much rain throughout the summer. Michael assessed my patch; and, anxious to begin the harvest, he decided we could bring a load of plants indoors and force them to finish under perfect conditions.

* * *

SEPTEMBER 10—*Michael, Tony and I snuck up the steep bank tonight and moved as many of my potted plants as we could. The roots had grown through the containers and into the hillside, making it difficult to tear them out. I had a bad feeling about this but did what I was told. We dragged the pots through the thick bush, down the hill and then scrambled to shove them through the side door of the basement. Daisy's wading pool and other containers in the house had been positioned under several grow lights. The trail of dirt from the patch to the house was like a highway, but the move was over in a few hours. Once again the floors in our house were covered with my favorite mixture of dirt and water.*

Every plant went into shock from the clumsy expedition. Nothing got bigger or riper; instead, the plants started to die from the moment of upheaval on. Our greed and impatience for bigger, harder, better buds had cost us dearly. Had the plants been left alone they would have matured just fine on their own, eventually.

I rounded up some help and clipped my indoor/outdoor crop. It was small, spongy and difficult to work with. I felt stupid for interfering with Mother Nature and welcomed any punishment coming my way. I had no desire to see or clip any more pot—and the harvest was just beginning.

* * *

OCTOBER 2—*We drove to the development property today to check on Cousin Jimmy. We broke through his security system—a heavy chain tied around two trees, held in place by a single lock with a strategically placed beer bottle hiding the key. Farther up the driveway, he's carved deep ruts in the road and filled them with beer bottles. I can't figure out if he put them there for security or if he's just saving up for a trip to the bottle depot. Anyway, we just drove around them.*

Jimmy had been squatting in a small travel trailer on the land for over a year. He shared his food with bears and squirrels and spent the majority of his days drinking beer on a makeshift deck he'd constructed out of old chunks of mismatched wood. Deliverance. He had also been growing pot—or trying to—without much success. Jimmy could never quite get it through his head that plants need water to survive. I'd have bet he had more money in returnable beer bottles than his marijuana crop would produce.

Rule number one was no growing marijuana on this property, and rule number two was no late mortgage or tax payments. Jimmy broke both of these fundamental rules inside the first six months. The land was in Jimmy's name because Michael owed Revenue Canada money. At this point, Jimmy had Michael over a barrel. All of our attempts to get in touch with him failed; he didn't respond to notes we left, and messages left with his family went unreturned. I didn't know what he was up to, but Michael thought it was bad.

* * *

Michael's patches were all doing well; but he only had part-time help from Willy, who lived several hours away. He convinced the longhaired teenager to hire a friend and work fulltime as guards for the remainder of the year. Michael hadn't been able to accommodate all his clones by planting time; he was exhausted and short a couple of hundred holes. Now forty years old and suffering from arthritis, he could only do so much on his own. The extra plants had all been repotted into large containers and tucked away in a secluded greenhouse. If Willy and his pal did a good job, the greenhouse would be their bonus.

The two longhaired nineteen-year-olds did a good job, all right. A good job at drinking and having huge bush parties with kids from their hometown on land they were meant to be guarding; a great job at smoking pot all day long and bingeing on cocaine when they could afford it. But the best thing they did was get fired.

Michael had given one of the two permission to take a night off;

the choice of who stayed behind on guard duty was theirs. Willy won the toss and left his friend Vern in charge of five hundred harvestable plants. Later that day, the two buddies ended up in their hometown, in the same nightclub, at the same time. Vern had snuck away after dark and hitchhiked for three hours, never expecting to run into Willy.

* * *

Willy looked at Vern in amazement. "What the fuck are you doing here, man?"

A drunken Vern stammered some stupid explanation through the void in his front teeth and concluded, "I guess if Michael finds out, we're dead."

"Damn right, we're dead, buddy. And it's your goddamn fault."

* * *

Vern never even bothered to come back. When Willy returned the following afternoon, hung over and tired, Michael was there to greet him—in a great mood after spending the night in his truck. He had gone to the property late the previous afternoon to pick up some spare tires and noticed the camp was deserted. He puttered around as he worked on possible speeches for the impending firings.

Willy was not really in shit, but Vern was most definitely fired. The neglect and death of the greenhouse got Willy fired a week later. That, and his constant need for days off and cash advances for booze, drugs and endless tattoos involving motorcycles and skulls.

Before Willy returned home, Michael paid him in full and lent him some money. A couple of months later, Willy's mother phoned and asked where her son's bonus was. When we explained that a bonus was for someone who worked hard and was dedicated, she still didn't get it. Michael said the bonus had dried up and died at the hands of Willy and Vern. Willy's mom then said her son wouldn't pay back the money he'd borrowed from Michael; that could serve as the bonus. As a result of this disagreement, Michael and Willy did not talk to each other for over a year.

Michael did a lot of hand-watering that year. He packed buckets through the bush virtually every day from May to September. His already tired and beat-up body took a lot of abuse; both his knees were injured and cysts developed in his hands. Two of his patches were watered with the system he'd designed the previous season for the Indian Reserve; this only required running at top speed through brambles and trees as the pump forced the water through hundreds of feet of hose.

On one of his solo missions near the end of October the water system scared away a charging black bear. Michael stood at the edge of a patch with no bear mace or weapon, just a limp, empty length of hose in his hand, waiting for the water. He heard brush cracking and rustling, and seconds later a large black bear emerged. It started running towards him after rearing onto its hind legs, sniffing the air. As Michael's life flashed before his eyes, he could hear the bear panting and smell its stench.

As the bear closed the gap between him and his intended target, the stunned grower's watering system engaged and jerked loudly to life. The hose stiffened and air and water shot out in loud, powerful spurts in the bear's direction. The timing was perfect. The animal stopped as abruptly as he had appeared and retreated. The entire incident probably lasted a minute, but it left Michael bothered for weeks. Growing alone was dangerous.

At the end of this draining season, we found our dream house. It was our one and only distraction from the all-consuming herb. We already owned a house, but I was tiring of isolation. I also found it frustrating and a great waste of time to have to drive for an hour and a half to get to a town. We lived in the wilderness yet owned only a small lot perched on a steep bank. Our land was useless, and the house had more than served its purpose. It had been purchased to grow in (and from and behind), and it had made us a lot of money.

We phoned the owner of the little house and farm we had fallen in love with and she told us it was not for sale. She did offer to keep our number, though, and call us if she ever decided to sell.

With the harvest finally in sight, Aunty Kenny offered his basement for clipping; so Michael rented it for two months. Kenny's crop was small, and he welcomed the company a clipping crew would bring. Sherry was in for another season and had become somewhat of a professional clipper over the last few years. She was due to arrive just after James. James returned after securing another leave of absence from his job in Whistler, and Rob Hudson begged us to put his wife Liza to work, promising amazing speed and dedication. I couldn't help picturing her tiny, blond head bent over the desk covered with cocaine; but Liza was very fit-looking and had a reputation for being an extremely hard worker.

She did prove to be truly amazing, but what was more incredible than her clipping speed was the fact that someone her size could ingest such large amounts of alcohol and drugs and still function. She worshiped Michael and loved working because it got her out of the house and away from Rob, whom she couldn't stand. Every time Liza got drunk, a guaranteed daily occurrence, she'd tell anyone who would listen about her plans to leave him. These plans usually involved a truck and camper, a few bottles of Kahlua and some sort of lesbian fling.

The pot started to flow into the clipping room in early October; the steady stream soon became a torrent, and Michael was on his way to his biggest year yet. With no partner or full-time employees left, Michael stood to make a good profit. I went to camp out at my parents' with Daisy. Mom and Dad looked after their grandchild while Carmella and I clipped Dad's pot. Six or seven large, beautiful plants were lost to a mysterious airborne fungus; the rest were harvested during the second month of an incredible Indian summer.

Carmella and I worked in the guesthouse and bothered my parents only for meals. My mother didn't know that Carmella was a vegetarian and provided healthy farm food, including meat in accordance with her size. This did not go over well at all. Carmella was mortally offended by the very smell of red meat. Like the Mormon who visits your house and is appalled when you offer her coffee, Carmella expected her hosts to anticipate and meet all her special needs with no advance notice. I felt no pity for her when my mother didn't run out and buy tofu and veggie patties. Carmella was offended but vowed to do her best, despite the harsh working conditions.

The job should have taken a week or so, but Carmella's special needs prevailed. One entire day was lost in the hunt for a specific rubber ring to go on a specific Turkish coffee pot. Only organic beans from a specific source could be used, and only Turkish stovetop coffee made from these would do. I drove around for three hours with an unbathed Carmella next to me and eventually got angry and suggested that maybe she could make do with regular coffee for a day or two. I had to roll down all the windows in my car just to keep from gagging.

Also required were special scissors, which most clippers would bring along to the job. We visited three sewing stores and looked over every pair of scissors until a German-made pair for $65 was chosen. Later, all dozy and stupid on pot, Carmella would sweep these same scissors into a pile of clippings and garbage on the floor and we would lose another twenty minutes looking for them.

I wanted to like Carmella, but I'd never met anyone who could push my buttons the way she did. One moment, she could be sweet and funny. The next, she'd engage me in a futile argument that no one could possibly win. It was like we were lovers in a dysfunctional relationship; we'd have a heated argument and then make up cautiously and carry on as if nothing had happened.

Sherry finally came to my rescue. She breezed into our clipping room in a crisp new floral dress, scissors in hand, and eyed up the situation immediately. As Carmella slunk down to the house for a piece of chocolate cake, Sherry simply said, "Well, I see nothing's changed with Carmella. Same shit, different year. I think maybe her ass is a bit bigger, though."

We wrapped up the job in two long days, and everyone returned home. Dad was told to check on the screens of drying buds and make sure the fans and heaters were running. He was specifically told to do nothing more.

A few days later, Michael, Daisy and I were at Michael's parents' cabin on the lake when Dad arrived for a visit. We all had lunch and relaxed on the porch enjoying a perfect, cloudless afternoon. Then

Dad sent me to get something out of his car. I opened the door to grab a newspaper off the dash, and the skunky stench released from inside overpowered me. There, in a bright orange garbage bag, was Dad's stinky, wet pot—sweating profusely after a long drive in the warm car. Like any other beginner, my father didn't grasp just how long it takes pot to dry. He'd weighed the bag with himself before driving over and was sure he had thirty-five pounds. Excited as hell, he had come to show us. If he had been stopped for speeding or a road check, my dear old dad would have spent the day in jail. Whatever possessed him to drag his loot all the way around the lake and down the Trans Canada Highway still remains a mystery that only he can answer.

Part of the reason we didn't want him touching anything was so he could see for himself how much the buds would shrink. Often, new growers believe they're being cheated if they don't see the whole drying process with their own eyes. My father would never think that we would cheat him, but it's hard to grasp the sad fact that marijuana is considered dry when eighty-five percent of its original weight is gone. We had to convince Dad that the huge clump of pot in the garbage bag was by no means dry, and certainly wouldn't weigh thirty-five pounds when it was. We skipped the lecture on driving around with all that dope in the car because, in a way, we were proud of Dad. He had obeyed the law all his life but saw our marijuana laws as archaic and silly. I was the daughter of a rebel.

James and Liza clipped and drank in Aunty Kenny's pot-saturated basement, Jimmy Buffet wailing his support through tinny speakers. Sherry came and went as her family obligations allowed, and the truckloads of raw marijuana were turned into tidy stacks of dried bud. October slipped away and soon it was Halloween. It was here, in a room full of dried and drying pot, with pumpkins flickering on the porch and skeletons hanging in the trees around our house, that Michael made James an offer he couldn't refuse.

James had expressed a lot of interest in growing for a year instead of just clipping; he thought it was something he'd really love to try. Michael proposed that James work a full year, from cloning in April or May right through to clipping in the fall. Instead of a partnership, which Michael wanted to avoid, James would be guaranteed seventy-five thousand dollars—more, if the year was spectacular. There was nothing to lose for James; he could count on a big payday and needed to invest nothing but time. He eagerly agreed.

Our buyer came from Alberta in early November with an advance to secure all of our pot—he paid only two thousand dollars per pound for the first time since 1992.

The advance was the exact amount we used as a down payment on our dream farm. The single mother of five who had rented the farm for the past year was driving the frail old owner crazy, and she was desperate to sell. The renter had bought a goat that had eaten most of the siding off the house and refused to pay rent because of the unauthorized "improvements" she'd been making. The place was overgrown and neglected, as its tenant was also busy making babies. In her last year on the farm, she had given birth to two premature babies within one calendar year. If this wasn't staggering enough, the babies were from two different fathers and joined three other fatherless boys between the ages of two and six.

This same tenant had convinced the owner to sign a contract stating that the only way to end the rental agreement would be upon the sale of the farm. We jumped at the opportunity to buy and immediately started planning our move.

Year Five, 1996

Defeat

I was so thrilled at the prospect of living on flat land, close to a town, that I didn't pay attention to the plans being laid. The Pot World thrives on fantasies and delusions of "next year"—which is always bound to be a better one. A pot grower without the ability to dream might as well kill himself or become a 7-Eleven employee of the month. My husband was plotting something grandiose, and I was completely oblivious to all of the signs.

Aunty Kenny came over for dinner one night; and, somehow, the conversation turned to pot.

"Have you guys seen the latest *High Times* magazine? My last show was better than anything I seen in there. My buds were just as big, just as juicy...I think that *I* should send in some pictures of this room that I have going right now. What do you think?"

Kenny's pot was always huge and impressive, but I thought the magazine was strictly for people who overused words like "dude" and "fine shit" and "killer herb." I also assumed that most of the readers smoked pot all day long out of huge bongs and showered twice a week at most. Intrigued, I wanted to help get Aunty Kenny what he wanted and see exactly what he was talking about.

I grabbed a couple of Michael's old issues of *High Times* and *Cannabis Canada*, thumbed through the pages and studied the winning photos. The pictures were always sent in by longhaired, sleepy-eyed dudes; and all the pictures looked the same to me: a great big bud with an explanation of what strain it was and how the dude grew such an awesome specimen. Sometimes, the photos included a scruffy dude in a greasy-looking T-shirt with a little blackout box over his eyes. I knew I could do better.

"Kenny, I think a winning picture should include a cute girl in sexy clothing, instead of all these hippie guys, *and* an incredible bud. I could be the girl and do my best to look sexy but not cheap or sleazy, and I could be holding the bud. Are you into trying that sort of approach?"

Aunty Kenny eagerly nodded his head in an enthusiastic yes, his blue eyes dancing with anticipation.

The next morning, I drove to Kenny's armed with my camera, a black silk push-up bra and some expensive sunglasses. Kenny had only one prop that he wanted me to include, a yardstick to prove the size of his really fine herb. We took fourteen pictures of me looking my poutiest amongst Kenny's totally huge buds. I wore the dark sunglasses in every photo, and Kenny made darn sure my breasts were included. We used the yardstick in four or five shots, supporting the impressiveness of Kenny's growing abilities.

Both Kenny and I were pleased with our amateur photo shoot and positive I'd be gracing the pages of *High Times* in the very near future. I drove home snickering to myself and feeling slightly exhilarated. I had never done anything of the sort in my entire life. I put my camera and sunglasses away until it was time to pack for Mexico several weeks later.

Michael and I owned several cameras; and like the excessive, capitalist pigs we had become, we took them all on our holiday. By the end of our first week, we had both shot a couple of rolls of film and decided to take them to the nearest town to have them developed.

"Hey, Princess, are the pictures that Kenny and you took on any of these films? Which camera did you guys use?"

I looked at the cameras lying on the bed and honestly couldn't remember which one I had given Kenny.

"I can't be sure, Michael. I'm sorry. Shit. Is it really that big a deal?"

Michael shrugged casually, not really concerned.

81

We both wanted to develop our film—Daisy was so incredibly cute in her little bathing suit and water wings—so, to be safe, I suggested that he take them in, as it was my face and half-exposed breasts that would be in the pictures. We went to a one-hour photo shop and "Jimmy Hendrix" dropped off several films while I hid up the street in a gift shop.

Two hours later we headed back to the photo shop. I remained a few stores away while Michael went alone to retrieve our pictures. Over the incessant drone of hungry vendors promising reams of crap for "almost free," I heard Michael calling my name, quietly at first and then louder and more urgently. The strangeness of his tone told me something was wrong.

I peered out onto the street from the safety of a tall pile of blankets and spotted him hurrying down the narrow sidewalk. As he got closer to me he explained that our photo shop was suddenly under police guard. There was an armed policeman in the entrance to the shop watching out the window, and another inside talking with the man behind the counter. I joined Michael on the street, and he grabbed my hand and led me through an alley. We started running.

We could only assume the police were there to extort money from the stupid Canadian tourists who dropped off a film full of marijuana photos. We literally ran the twelve blocks to the bus stop and grabbed the first bus back to our seaside villa. Once safely inside, we made a pact to never again photograph a marijuana plant, even if it was thirty feet tall, followed us home and said, "Hey, take my picture, will you?"

So, Aunty Kenny never got his wish, and I did not become a supermodel fantasy for an army of dreadlocked dudes stoned on bongs of really fine herb. We finished our holiday in relative peace and gladly returned home.

* * *

We were comfortable and happy in our new place, but it was very small. The bathroom was essentially in the kitchen, there wasn't one closet in the entire house and every time Michael went into Daisy's bedroom, he hit his head on the doorframe. There was no room for

James or anyone else in our humble abode. Just the thought of an alcoholic with permanent bad breath shitting inches away from my kitchen was enough for me to convince Michael that the place for James was anywhere but our tiny house. We fixed up our favorite outbuilding and awaited James's arrival.

The magic number for this year was to be a shocking four thousand plants.

"What? Four *thousand?* Are you out of your fucking mind? Where are you going to put four thousand plants, let alone clip them? And why do you need so many? Why are you so driven to make the big score? You're fucking crazy, and I want nothing to do with four thousand pot plants! What was I thinking when I married a pot grower?"

I stormed out of the house and walked down to the barn. When I needed to think, I enjoyed crawling up into the hayloft of our old barn and sitting with one of the cats. The sweet smell of the hay and the warmth of a cat on my lap always calmed me and helped put things into perspective.

If Michael didn't make a lot of money, we couldn't finish paying for our farm and buy the llamas we had been talking about raising. I got to stay at home with Daisy and go on winter holidays and drive a new vehicle and live with a wonderful man who loved me; I actually had it pretty good. I put down the big tomcat I had been snuggling and hurried down the ladder. I was ready to hear Michael's plans for the year.

Michael had done a lot of research and made preparations for the purchase of mass quantities of supplies. Rob Hudson, still crack-free at this point, had a friend named Ted who worked for the Ministry of Forests. Ted showered Michael with impressive-looking maps and drawings. He agreed to supply growing areas free of grazing cattle and silviculture with a year-round water source. The areas were to be of suitable altitude with decent road access. For this golden information, Michael would shell out twenty percent of his net profit at the end of the year. Rob and Mr. Forestry would split that in half.

On a chilly day in May, James putted into the yard in his antique MG. He was trim and fit, with short-cropped gray hair and, of course,

Polo pants and shirt.

"How's my favorite family?" he asked as he hugged us all warmly. "Are we ready to grow some dope, there, Boss Man?"

He reached into his car and pulled out an enormous packsack. He patted Michael on the back enthusiastically as we wandered across the yard. We showed James to his new home, which he loved; and he and Michael discussed their plans for the year.

Shortly afterwards, the mass cloning began. Every day, James and Michael would disappear into the crawl space under part of our house. Michael couldn't stand up straight at all because the maximum height of the ceiling was less than six feet. There were remnants of an attempted grow room left behind by the baby-producing tenant. Our mother plants were tucked away here, leaving the remainder of the tiny basement for clones. In only a few days, it became obvious there wasn't enough room. The first greenhouse of many was built to house the growing number of babies.

On May 29 a police car drove into the yard, and a young officer got out and approached the front door. We had a standing joke that included loud knocks on the door and someone saying, "Open up! It's the police!" Michael was constantly bullshitting everyone about everything, so I paid no attention when the knock on the door came. But this time, it really was the police; and it was James who spotted the car in the driveway.

Covered in dirt and water and with muddy, black hands, James was blindly running around the house dumping trays of clones into the flower beds and yelling, "Boss Man, the cops are here! What do we do?"

By the time we found Michael, the naive young cop was gone— after returning a license plate that had fallen off our utility trailer. He simply left the plate on the front porch with his card on top of it.

James's adrenaline was permanently in high gear from that day on; he never fully recovered from the shock. Michael and I thought him a tad paranoid for a full-time grower, his daily ritual of marijuana and booze consumption heightening his fears. He worked hard, though, and never questioned Michael; and the spring progressed smoothly.

Michael bought a heavy-duty posthole auger and half a semi truckload of baled potting soil. He bought new tools, camping gear, two-way radios, an all-terrain vehicle, a generator and tons of fertilizer. Our yard looked like a garden supply warehouse. James and Michael needed more help, and another old friend—and alcoholic—was hired.

Darcy had recently obtained his realtor's license, but he hadn't made a sale in his first six months. He was charming and attractive and always looked more ready to show a house than work in the bush. His hair had this incredible poofy quality, and James's Polo collection paled next to Darcy's. With Michael, James and Darcy all being older, a young, strong laborer was necessary to round out the team.

Adam, the boyfriend of Sherry's daughter April, was hired immediately. He was enthusiastic, energetic and the classic tall, dark and handsome. He also had a great sense of humor and did impersonations. Adam was pumping gas part-time for minimum wage and jumped at the opportunity to quadruple his wages and learn about growing. Young and madly in love, he and April were inseparable. They made the move to our area together, staying with us until Michael's old bus was livable. Michael's team was complete.

The building James inhabited had by now become mockingly known as the Love Shack. Every day after work he anxiously asked if his girlfriend had called. And every day I had to tell him that she had not. It wasn't because he had moved away to grow pot for a year; it was because she was having an affair. She was fifteen years younger than James and making a complete fool out of him. She never returned his phone calls and made flimsy excuses not to visit him—I have diarrhea, I have a headache, I have a doctor's appointment, I can't drive that far, etc. But she lived in James's house and drove his vehicle and spent his money while he moped and worried away his free time alone in the Love Shack.

James became more depressed and withdrawn over his failing relationship. With his girlfriend hundreds of miles away, there wasn't much he could do to improve things. Liquor was the only thing that numbed and temporarily cheered him up. And I had come to have almost no tolerance for drunks.

When Darcy and James got drinking together, it was a scary sight. Their last binge at our house had ended with Darcy sitting in the dark in our cramped kitchen, by himself, having a two-sided conversation. James made his way into his pit with darkened windows and unwashed sheets, leaving Darcy alone in the house. His smoldering cigarette burned his hand and then my new floor, the beginning of the end as far as I was concerned.

The next morning, Michael and I had a huge fight. I awoke to a kitchen littered with empty cans and bottles and a hole melted in the flooring.

"I've put up with moody Tony, drunken Willy, weird Herman, sloppy Jimmy, disgusting Ronnie and a barrage of other displaced losers! I have fed and housed them all while trying to raise our baby, and I am fucking fed up!"

The months of filthy laundry, beer cans, dirty dishes and endless conversations about pot were something I could no longer endure, not to mention the utter lack of privacy.

"I want Darcy gone, and Adam and April can move to the property now!" I demanded.

Michael agreed. He didn't even argue with me and said he would speak to everyone immediately. By noon, only Daisy and I remained in the house. I scrubbed and vacuumed, opened all the windows and filled the house with clean, fresh air. The clothesline was full of bedding and towels with that incredible outdoor-fresh smell, and I knew that our employee boarding house was permanently closed.

* * *

MAY 25—*My llamas arrived today! They are so beautiful—fuzzier than I had imagined with huge, dark eyes and long graceful necks. They aren't very snuggly, though; I'll have to work on that. Michael and I agree that there is a similarity in aloofness to that of a cat. I love a challenge over the submissive suckiness of a pet like a dog. Now, we have a farm.*

The first order of business was the digging of four thousand holes. The auger broke down regularly and ate through four drill bits; but after two weeks of steady digging, the final tally was thirty-six hundred. Two guys would run the auger, one of whom was always Michael, while the others scooped loose dirt out of the fresh holes. Then the holes were camouflaged and filled with sterile soil, fertilizers and water crystals. Each patch contained about one hundred holes five or six feet apart, according to Michael's discretion. With a drive of up to three or four hours one-way and heavy supplies to drag through the bush, a good day would be two hundred completed holes. Then each patch would be visited again with clones to be planted, watered in and protected from chewing critters.

Things were basically going well. The only real problem to speak of was Darcy. One hot, sticky evening, after a hard day digging holes, the team grabbed a couple of cheap motel rooms for the night. The exhausted crew dined on greasy burgers and beer and checked into their respective orange-and-brown-shag-carpeted rooms. Michael had a long, hot shower and went straight to bed. He assumed that everyone else had done the same, but the truth was a different matter. All three employees sneaked out to the pub while the boss slept soundly.

James and Darcy, both professional alcoholics, outlasted young Adam, who crawled back to Michael's room around one in the morning. At five, Michael woke up and rousted Adam, whom he sent next door to wake the sleeping drunks.

Adam returned empty-handed, a frown on his tanned young face. He did a quick impression of James and Darcy, cross-legged, drunk and smoking cigarettes; but even this couldn't cheer Michael out of the dark mood that was settling over him. Darcy had piled all the furniture in the room against the door so no one could get in and wake him. He refused to answer the phone or respond to loud, angry knocks; and half a day was lost because of this performance. At one o'clock in the afternoon when Darcy finally got up, he felt no guilt and actually thought it was funny.

Michael's budget was so out-of-control already he saw no humor in having to pay people to stand around and wait for someone who was sleeping. When they finally got to work that day, everyone was so hung over that it was almost impossible to work in the hot sun and droning insects.

Darcy's sleaziness knew no boundaries. He stole money out of the work truck for booze and cigarettes and probably got away with it for a while. Smooth and salesman-like, he somehow implicated Adam in the missing money, which Michael had recently noticed. Eventually, James and Michael figured out just what had been happening, and that it was not Adam but Darcy. He was quietly let go. No fuss was made—he'd been hired temporarily and was no longer needed. Michael was so happy to get rid of him. Darcy had been a wonderful man who was losing himself to alcohol and becoming a real piece of shit.

All of the new areas were drilled and ready for planting fairly close to schedule. By the end of June, all the holes had been filled. The weary but jovial crew finished one of the last areas and headed down a bumpy, overgrown logging road. There, directly in their path, just up the road, was a transport truck. The truck was full of cattle, which had been guaranteed not to be there. So, the crew sat and watched as the entire herd of mooing, shitting cows stumbled out of the truck and thrashed through the bush. A newly planted patch of three hundred was dangerously close. The truckload of exhausted pot growers continued home as the cattle truck backed off the road. All they could do was hope the cows didn't do too much damage.

The next visit revealed not damage but full-blown disaster. It wasn't that cows ate marijuana; they trampled it and shit on it while looking for suitable grazing. Ted was in for a piece of Michael's mind.

It wasn't terribly surprising when, a week or two later, a maintenance visit in an area of eight hundred went bad. This patch had been in for over a month and was doing well. Michael's favorite strain was flourishing.

Michael and James unloaded supplies while Adam lit a cigarette. As he leaned up against the truck admiring the landscape, he noticed something out of place.

"Hey, James, was that string here last time we were up here?"

"String? What string? What are you talking about, Junior?"

And there it was, the complete ruination of another huge area. Miles of forestry string was running right through the middle of the patch. This meant that the block of land —including our dope—was slated for logging or thinning or tree planting. It also meant that someone else would probably be harvesting our hard-earned crop. Michael decided that, after he killed the asshole who had fucked up two of his guaranteed areas, he would dig up and move the plants. James voiced his disapproval for this plan, but Michael reminded him of his guarantee. Michael set aside several days for the relocation of three hundred plants.

We borrowed my father's hay trailer and started the arduous relocation project. Each plant was gently dug up with a small shovel and placed in a large plastic tub filled with dirt. The tubs were carried out of the bush and placed in the back of the truck. The load was then concealed and driven to a new location where new holes had been prepared. After several exhausting trips, the plants had a new home. But, as luck would have it, the worst was far from over.

The next problem was in the grow zone farthest from our home, the one near where Darcy had barricaded himself in the motel room. Michael, Adam and James, who by now was suffering from two bad knees, made the long drive together and planned on giving the plants an organic foliar fertilizer known as Rocket Fuel. The ingredients basically smelled like rotten shit, were expensive and hard to find. The patch was also hard to find—because most of it was gone. Out of eight hundred plants, there were maybe a hundred left. Something had killed them, leaving only small, wilted remains on the ground near the holes.

This was strange, because usually plants are either eaten or chewed on, suffering from some sort of diagnosable problem obvious with a quick look or completely dead. This time, no one had any idea what could have caused the massive massacre of marijuana.

Feeling pissed off and defeated, the loser growers sat down and stared despondently at what had been the best and biggest patch. A welcome summer wind rustled through the meadow, drying the sweat off their bodies as they tried to digest the extent of the latest disaster. They thought of all the hours of sweat and grunt work that had gone into making the waste land before them a beautiful garden.

It was as they were sitting quietly, conquered, a high pitched whistling swept through the forest among the trees. As the breeze died down, the forest became quiet.

"Junior, did you hear that?" James poked Adam in the side and turned his head in the direction of the sound. "I thought I heard someone whistling."

"Yeah. I heard that. What the hell is it?" Adam wondered aloud.

"Gophers," answered Michael. "It's gophers that have slaughtered us."

A fat golden gopher scurried across the hillside and disappeared into a pile of brush.

"Fuck. I thought I'd seen it all. Well, at least we know what it is now." Michael put his head in his hands and shook it slowly.

As the gophers tunneled through the newly planted pot patch, they found tender roots that led to fresh, juicy greens. The summer had been hot and dry, and the indigenous vegetation was parched. Michael's patch of marijuana was an oasis for many small rodents. The fertilizing was postponed as they made plans to go to war with the gophers.

Michael never killed animals. This was the only time I ever knew him to engage in any sort of hunting or killing. After driving home depressed, with another patch annihilated, he read up on how to kill gophers, moles, marmots and ground squirrels and stocked up on smoke bombs and ammunition.

Scads of stunned gophers scampered out of their smoky burrows into an onslaught of bullets from the awaiting .22. Bang! Bang! Bang! Bang! Furry, little corpses littered the ground and joined hundreds of marijuana plants in the dance of death. Michael felt sick to his stomach as he pulled the trigger and lined up another gopher in the scope of the rifle. He couldn't do it. He couldn't kill one more rodent even if it cost him the rest of the patch. That day would be the only day of gopher killing.

The slaughter had left Michael physically sick, and the subsequent guilt that ate at his guts was worse. He vowed to let nature take its course and lose the rest of the patch, if necessary. He also decided to really baby the remaining plants and headed to his "guaranteed water source."

"Boy, that Ted sure knows his areas!" he yelled sarcastically. "What a lowdown little prick. I don't think this guy even works for Forestry—maybe he works in the building, as a janitor or something. I'm fucked. Cows, gophers, string and now this—no water. In fucking July. My kid could have found me better areas, and I wouldn't owe her twenty percent!"

By now it was obvious that Rob and Michael had been lied to. Ted must have gambled that things like grazing rights and active logging in such a vast area were few and far between. The creek supplying water for the entire area had quit flowing and dried up; there was no sign of anything remotely wet and it was only July 20th. This was a disaster.

Rocket Fuel had to be mixed in water, as did many fertilizers and fungicides. After searching for most of the day, Michael found a water source. It was eight miles from the patch on an impossibly bad road and straight uphill. Even Big Blue couldn't do it. Michael tipped the truck over full of water and had to dump the load to get out. The plants were officially on their own—if the heat wave continued, they would all be dead by the end of the week.

What everyone wanted by now was Rob's friend with the bad information dead by the end of the week. Michael wrote off the patch in his mind and recalculated his projected earnings. Adam had cost an extra fifteen thousand dollars already and most of the areas were in some kind of trouble. James's guarantee became the subject of many late-night husband-and-wife discussions.

Of course, I had been led to believe the amount James had been promised was fifty thousand dollars. Partway through the season, James quietly told Michael he had promised twice that much. I completely freaked out; and, finally, the two men settled on seventy-five thousand, which I think had been the original amount they'd agreed to all along. Michael honestly couldn't remember what he had

91

promised. He did know the time to make a financial decision is not when one is standing knee-deep in pot. The rest of the season was carried out with James's impending guarantee hanging over our heads like a gloomy thundercloud.

We did have Michael's property loaded with plants, as usual. Nothing had ever really gone wrong there, other than my and Jimmy's over-use of fertilizer. The hot holes had been cleaned out and neutralized and four hundred new holes dug. The plants were huge, the strain given to us by the same guy that had provided me with my first years' giants. There was some consolation in this.

Michael wanted a few days alone to rest and regroup, so James returned home to Whistler to see his doctor and try to patch up his relationship. His knees had become full of tiny bone splinters due to years of extreme snowboarding and skiing. Hiking on rough terrain laden with heavy supplies was exacerbating his condition.

James came back refreshed physically; but, mentally, he had deteriorated. His girlfriend had finally admitted she had been sleeping with some young, hotshot skier with a budding career in Warren Miller films. James was devastated.

One morning after breakfast, James confessed to Michael that he'd had a vision. There, in his humble, sad Love Shack, an angel had visited him. The angel was male, with white hair, and had spoken to James from the end of his bed. All I remember is the disgust and anger in Michael's face as he stormed into the house.

"Princess, I don't think I can take any more this year. Our wonderful employee thinks he just saw a fucking angel. Can you believe it? An angel. He says it had white hair and appeared to him at the end of the bed. I think he's lost his fucking mind." Michael paced our tiny kitchen pointing out the window to the building James inhabited. "I'll tell you one thing, one angel's the limit. If he sees one more fucking angel or anything else in there, he's gone. I've got you and a small child to think about. You live at my house, you get one chance to see an angel. Any more sightings and I'll ask him to leave. I think he's completely unstable. It must be the booze finally catching up with him."

"Really, you'd kick him out? You can't ask him to leave; it's not like he's dangerous or anything. He's just depressed. Calm down," I urged.

"Total fucking godhead—one more vision, and I'll send him packing!" Michael was also suffering mentally. He was wound so tight that one more screw-up from anyone around him could completely unravel what was left of his sanity.

Convinced he'd had a spiritual experience, the once fun-loving drunk became quiet and withdrawn. James was thin and tired-looking, the skin on his face an unhealthy shade of yellow. He was definitely changed after the vision. Michael gave him a pet project at home to distract him from the angel and his cheating ex-girlfriend. In his divine stupor, he hardly heard what Michael was telling him. He woke up early the next morning and headed to the back field, where he was preparing to carry out an experiment for the Boss Man.

Michael figured that if he planted small clones late in the year they would just have time to go into bud and be miniature, single colas. A *cola* is the top, main branch or bud on a marijuana plant. It contains the highest concentration of THC, the chemical that produces the high. Small plants grown this way would require no camouflage or tying down because they wouldn't be visible from the air.

James worked the ground with a pitchfork until it was smooth and weed-free. The experimental garden was just the thing to get his mind back in focus, and he took pride in making the project perfect.

* * *

AUGUST 15—*I've been summoned to replace Darcy. My job is unbearable. Michael makes me stand, like a stationary tin soldier, watching for vehicles. Blood on the moon would be a more likely occurrence than traffic in this desolate piece of wilderness, and the cold is so intense that no amount of running on the spot could warm me. I am also terrified of bears and he knows it—probably grizzlies or polar bears in this country. As I stand guard, Michael and Adam fertilize and spray for mold while James mans the*

93

*pump in the truck, his knees no longer able to carry
him through the bush.*

My first night out, on the way home, James sat on a can of bear mace
that just happened to have the safety off. The entire contents of the
can discharged into the cab of the truck, temporarily blinding him.

"Jesus Christ! What the hell is going on back there, Mary-Ann?"
Adam yelled.

"It's him, it's James. Shit, he's set off the bear mace in his pants."
I started laughing as I looked over at James's face. Most of the spray
had ended up on his Polo shorts and fleece coat; but as he squirmed
in an attempt to stop the stream of pepper, more of the spray shot
from the can. He was utterly bewildered, let down by his angel and
certain about the abuse he was going to take over this.

Every one of us received a blast of the pepper somewhere, with
James and Adam getting hit the worst. We all jumped from the
uninhabitable truck until enough time had passed to air it out. This
story became a running joke on James; and it was fitting that it was
he, alone on guard one afternoon, and not me who encountered a
bear.

* * *

A frenzied voice came over the radio. "Oh, God! I see a bear, and it's
pretty close. Michael, do you read me? What do I do? What do I do?"

Michael was by the truck, half a mile away, running the pump and
offered very little help. "Just stay calm, James. What's the bear doing?
Can it see you?"

"Oh, shit! Oh, shit! He's running towards me—I think he sees me.
What should I do?"

"How close is he?"

"Real fucking close! What should I do, Michael?"

Michael's only words of advice: "Run, you idiot! Run!"

What James had failed to mention was that he was kneeling. When
he stood up and started running the bear stopped abruptly, turned
and headed in a different direction. It had probably never even seen

him crouched behind a bushy fir tree.

This story soon became the favorite, with James the brunt of the joke, again. That was, until James and Adam went drinking in town together one night.

I went out to the Love Shack one morning to roust James for work.

"I just need to put my head back on the pillow for a bit, and I'll be as good as new."

But four or five hours went by before he was able get out of bed. I did his work in the field and knocked on his door again around dinnertime. A sheepish, bruised and stinky James appeared in the doorway, his face almost unrecognizable.

"Jesus, James. What happened to your face? I think you might have to see a doctor about this, or at least let me have a look at you. Come up to the house."

His right eye was dark purple and swollen completely shut and the rest of his face cut in deep, bloody cracks. His hands were cut up and puffy, but he assured me that the worst things were his cracked ribs—he was unable to laugh, cough or smoke pot. We washed his cuts with disinfectant and put butterfly bandages on two of the more serious wounds. I bandaged his ribs and cleaned his hands in a sink of warm water and Epsom salts, horrified at his distended face.

"I assure you, Mary-Ann, the other guy is in far worse shape. Me and Junior make quite the tag team." James attempted to laugh but instead winced in pain, doubling over and holding his torso with his good hand.

Our Hundred-Thousand-Dollar Man, as I called him, now had two bad knees, one eye, fractured ribs, a bad case of depression and divine intervention going on in the Love Shack. It was a good thing that most of the plants were dead.

We gave James a few days off to heal, and then it was back to work. Although it was only August, some of the plants near the cow zone were ready to harvest. The buds were small but tight and full of reddish-brown hairs. We managed to bring seventy plants out one day, working harder than ever to get them to the truck. The road had been deactivated, forcing us to travel on foot shouldering heavy garbage bags over huge mounds of dirt placed intentionally to stop traffic. The plants were brought home and clipped while we planned another trip to the area.

We headed out early on a perfect fall morning. The air was crisp; and a heavy dew had blanketed our yard, wetting everything with its cool, pure moisture. I walked to the fence and received a warm nuzzle from Felix, my friendliest llama. I inhaled as deeply as I could, in awe of nature's seductive brilliance, before I settled in the truck. We drove to the patch, entertained by Adam's latest impression of his "brother-in-law," and hid the truck in a small clearing near the start of the roadwork.

As we approached the first plot of two hundred, it was obvious from a distance that something was terribly wrong. The plants looked like sticks, like something had stripped them of all of their fan leaves. Fan leaves are the specific leaves that were gone—also called guard leaves, they take the brunt of any punishment or nutrient and then supply or protect the rest of the plant. They were shadows of what they had been only days before.

"Oh, God, they look like little green baseball bats. Holy fuck-dogs! This isn't good, guys," giggled Michael.

"It's just one patch, Mike," Adam said softly, his face suggesting that he shared the panic that was welling up inside me.

"Frost doesn't just hit one patch; it hits the whole mountain," Michael said solemnly.

Every plant was frozen solid and turning to mush as the sun hit the first patch. A freak frost, and it was only August. There were hardly any plants left in the wild grow areas, and now this one was gone, too. Every patch seemed to have been systematically wiped out. We hiked through the bush and made our way to all the patches in the area; the disaster was all-encompassing. Not one plant lived to be harvested.

Michael and I wondered aloud about the elevation of these areas.

"I always found it so cold and barren when you had me stand guard up here. What's the elevation of these particular patches, anyway?"

Ted the liar had been wrong about almost everything else, and now we doubted the elevation at all of his areas.

"I was starting to wonder about that lately, but the areas had all been planted. I just hoped for the best, but I think Ted has fucked me again. I'll buy an altimeter watch and come back out here tomorrow," Michael promised. "I don't think we're going to like what we find."

We learned that the elevation in the first frosty patch was forty-seven hundred feet. At that altitude, we should have been raising llamas and not marijuana. The other areas weren't much better. Never before had Michael been so completely taken in, or felt so stupid and gullible. Every promise Ted had made turned out to be a lie. Michael drove to Rob's to inform him of the latest disaster.

All we had left were the giants at Michael's acreage. Oddly, they were showing no signs of maturity; this led to an investigation of epic proportions. From expert to idiot, everyone we knew who grew marijuana was questioned. What were we to do with four hundred plants that were ten or twelve feet tall and had no hairs or buds on them? We had been growing long enough and read enough marijuana books to know only one thing for certain—we were in trouble.

Michael went to the owner of the strain, who had been camped out for most of the season and unreachable. The poor guy had planted over two thousand of the giants himself, and none showed any signs of finishing. The devastating conclusion was that someone had mixed up indoor mothers with outdoor mothers. The clones that Michael and his clone provider had planted were an indoor strain and not likely to come off in Canada. Not one to give up easily, Michael began researching ways to encourage marijuana to bud. We should have known from previous experience that messing with Mother Nature doesn't work.

One of our illustrious pot middles, a guy named Tim who never brushed his teeth, told us to put a brown paper bag over part of each plant. This was meant to signal darkness to the plant and tell it to go immediately into bud. This method was the lesser of two evils. The only other feasible suggestion was to cloak each plant entirely with dark cloth every afternoon at a specific time and pull the cloths off in the morning. The only problem was that we had four hundred plants, all over eight feet high and four feet wide.

My father, although not relying on pot for income, had also bought fifty clones from us that spring because he'd had such a good time growing his first crop that he wanted to do it again. He noticed that things in his garden looked a lot different from the previous year; we felt responsible for his imminent failure.

I was sent to Costco to purchase five hundred lunch-size brown paper bags. The desperate crew then went to the patch and secured the bags to a branch of each plant with a twist tie. Oh, the sight of it—a piece of property covered in enormous indoor marijuana plants, each decked out in her own paper bag. It rained, the sun shone, wind ripped through the forest, it rained some more and, eventually, the paper bags started to tatter. Still no sign of buds.

* * *

OCTOBER 10—*The days have become colder and shorter, and still our plants show no signs of maturing. The deteriorating paper bags have ripped away from their twist ties and blown all over the forest, getting caught in trees and brambles. I have no idea how we're going to pay James. This year has been a disaster. I'd give anything to be nursing again and have a paycheck every two weeks. Michael is on edge, though he hides it pretty well. We talk about how to pay James and make our mortgage payments every day. James is going home tomorrow. He's happy to go back to Whistler, but I can feel his disappointment in his year as a grower.*

In late October, Michael wrote the entire paper bag area off. Stubborn and optimistic, my dad refused to have paper bags tied to his plants and, instead, hired young Adam to dig up his ten best plants and move them indoors. He was convinced that the plants would flourish inside and reward him for his patience.

At Dad's request, Michael and I converted my parents' guesthouse to a grow room. Adam dug up ten massive plants, and Dad hauled them to their new home with a tractor. Michael and I set up the room so it would be foolproof and gave Dad a detailed list of instructions. He fed and watered his plants on schedule but pulled the timers out of the wall, baffled by unfamiliar technology, refusing to even try them.

Every day, Dad would stroll up to the guesthouse in his threadbare blue bathrobe and check on his room. He would turn the lights on manually, admiring the profitable indoor garden before him. Some days he'd arrive at his room at eight, some days at nine; and, often, if he had insomnia and got up really early, he'd go up at six and switch on the four one-thousand-watt lights. In the evening, the procedure was repeated—minus the blue bathrobe.

No one told us this until the room had been in for a few weeks, and the plants started looking really weird. They were in bud and full of new growth all at the same time. We were totally puzzled until the day my mother inadvertently spilled the beans.

"He never goes up there at the same time, you know, Mary-Ann. Your father is a funny, funny man. Sometimes he sits around in that awful blue housecoat until nine or ten o'clock before he finally goes out and does his thing. I've told him to follow the schedule and listen to what you've told him about the timers, but you know how stubborn he is."

Problem solved! The first rule of indoor growing is twelve hours of uninterrupted darkness every day while the plants are in their budding stage. There can be not so much as a sliver of light in the room during the dark hours, or the plants think spring is coming and start to grow or vegetate. Dad's plants were very confused. They didn't know what to think, yet still he refused to use the timers, believing them to be unnatural and somehow inaccurate.

Michael drove over one day and hooked everything up to the two timers, only to find them unhooked at his next visit. Dad was lectured thoroughly and agreed to leave the timers when we threatened him with the possibility of no crop and no help.

"Dad, I can't take any more shit with this room of yours! I would rather scrape Tim's teeth clean with my fingers than clip your stressed-out pot, alone, in that room, at Christmas. It's got to stop!"

I drew the line at Dec. 21st, and that's when I finally took the room down. Dad ended up with three and a half of the fluffiest, ugliest pounds I've ever seen. He never grew pot—or anything else—again.

We were forced to build a makeshift indoor room at home. What little pot we had that didn't freeze or disappear was not enough to pay the bills *and* James's guarantee. Prices for outdoor had dropped another two hundred dollars per pound to eighteen-hundred dollars. And, if that wasn't bad enough, our buyer had developed a drug problem and wanted everything fronted, a potentially disastrous way of selling pot. It seemed as if every second person we met had become a pot grower, and the market was flooded. We gave our meager amount of pot to the budding addict and crossed our fingers.

Luckily, Michael had some plants in buckets. They were a late strain and only partly developed, but there were enough of them to warrant an effort. Hoping to squeeze an extra ounce or two out of each plant, Michael piled them all into the back of his truck and drove them home.

Before moving the plants inside, renovations to James's former home were necessary. We emptied the pickup onto the lawn and hurried inside to set up the room. Michael sent me outside to start bringing plants in—and there was Felix, munching on marijuana leaves. A fan leaf dangled casually from his rubbery lips as he approached me for a routine kiss.

"Bad llama," I whispered as I shooed him away and grabbed all of the pots nearest the fence line—but the damage was done. Highly curious and willing to eat almost anything green, Felix had digested a considerable amount of pot. His sidekick Eddy hid behind the barn under his favorite tree, watching intently. Knowing that Michael would appreciate Felix's mischievousness, I called him outside. The green llama slime on my cheek and the stubs of the potted plants sent Michael into a welcome burst of laughter.

Our room turned out even worse than Dad's. The plants had some kind of disease that exploded once they were inside the warm, moist environment. Michael photographed the room and sent copies to

James to prove he wasn't trying to get out of paying the guarantee. We had actually lost money, spent all that we'd saved and were still short twenty thousand dollars for James. Our seemingly unpoppable bubble of money had burst and showered us with disappointing reality.

* * *

> DECEMBER 27—*At this point, I hate the Pot World more than anything I've ever hated. I feel helpless and stupid. I want out! It's not working for us anymore—we're going backwards. We seem to be trapped in a web of deceit and debt and lust for money. The biggest drag is having to lie to everyone we meet—friends, family members, strangers. And the guilt associated with selling drugs is eating away at me. I'm always scared that people can smell me or sense that I'm involved in the drug world. I know that pot is just an herb and almost harmless, as far as drugs go…but it's illegal. I'm having a much harder time with that than Michael.*

Getting out of this world would be much harder than nonchalantly sliding in; so many shady people now knew what we did and could turn us in at any time. Michael honestly still loved growing and everything about it, which put a strain on our relationship. When things frustrated the hell out of me and I felt that I had no control over my life, I'd look to Michael for support. But he viewed the whole picture differently.

Michael never wavered or thought about changing professions. He justified every aspect of our life and illegal career. Every year we filed income tax and contributed to society as best we could.

"There are *no* jobs for forty-five-year-old bartenders with an eleventh grade education" was his standard reply to all arguments pot-related. There was no hospital or similar facility for me to work in, and Daisy was thriving and happy right where she was. We didn't suck anything out of an already financially exhausted social service system; we were independent entrepreneurs. And, morally, we saw nothing wrong with the herb we were growing and had both become all for the legalization of pot. If we quit growing, we'd have to sell our dream farm and move to a city to find work. That was something we both agreed we absolutely couldn't do. And that was what kept us in the sticky, blanketing web of dope growing.

Michael had just pulled off his worst year; James offered no sympathy. He said he'd have no problem waiting for the rest of his money; he knew the Boss Man was good for it. No problem waiting to get paid...well, that was reassuring. It was hard to guarantee anything out of nothing, and nothing was what we had.

With Michael a little disillusioned with the Pot World and 1996 almost behind us, I suggested I try my hand at an indoor room. We needed to come up with the rest of James's payment, and Michael had been growing for years now without a break. I consulted Aunty Kenny, and he suggested a strain he had been growing with great success. I would do the room in dirt as opposed to hydroponics, just to keep things simple, and have some money rolling in shortly.

Kenny was no rocket scientist or specialized botanist, and he did wear chains on his rubber boots; so I figured I'd be guaranteed success. I cleaned and rearranged the Love Shack and got down to work. Every day I strolled down to the shack and entered my own private Pot World. The grow room was sunny and warm, with a modest four lights and twenty lovely clones from Aunty Kenny. I enjoyed the indoor garden, and if not for the insipid humming of the ballasts I could often believe I was out in the forest on a summer day. The only remnant of James was the Polo shirt he had been beaten up in that I used as a rag. I could almost taste success.

The formula was simple: a day of water followed by a day of fertilizer, followed by a day of water and so on. The only other thing I had to do was empty the reservoirs the buckets sat in and turn the plants periodically. Everything looked great for about a month. The plants were huge and nicely into bud, and I was counting the pounds and adding up the money. I loved growing pot!

Of course, something evil had been there all along, but I'd been too busy patting myself on the back to notice—nasty, dreaded, plant-sucking spider mites. Not just a few bugs but a full-blown colony. The world within the walls of the Love Shack was now theirs.

I sprayed chemicals until my lips and hands were numb and my lungs burned. I even crawled around on my hands and knees to get the undersides of each individual leaf with bug-killing potions. I pulled off heavily infested fan leaves and sterilized the building with bleach and an array of other cleaners and pesticides.

Everything I sprayed on my dying plants just barely kept the bugs at bay. In a final act of desperation, I tried to hose the mites off the plants with water, but nothing seemed to be going my way. The hose kept getting kinked and tangled, buckets tumbled over and I tripped and fell into the horse trough full of water that served as my reservoir. I dragged myself out of the cold, slimy water, soaked and humiliated, and launched into a tantrum fraught with swearing and hose- and plant-smashing. Oh, how I hated growing pot!

A bulb burst as the hose full of cold water flew from my hand, the explosion bringing me back to reality. Shivering and on the verge of tears, I surveyed the room—a huge mess of glass, dirt, water and broken branches. The only healthy thing in the building was the colony of spider mites. I went to get Michael.

"What *is* this, some kind of joke? I thought you said you knew what you were doing. How long have you had these mites?" Michael stepped inside and took a good, long look at the room. "Total fucking godhead, we're fucked. You might as well start clipping. They're not going to get any better. Jesus, Hon., what a fucking nightmare."

With his shoulders hunched and his head bowed in wife-cursing defeat, Michael photographed the Love Shack to show James what a disaster I'd made of things.

* * *

DECEMBER 30— *We had really been counting on the money from the Love Shack, and I have let everyone down. How can we so consistently fuck up something as simple as gardening? I believe there is a lesson in all of this—forces that we cannot control are saying "enough is enough." I give up. Michael and I are becoming distant. He is depressed, and I am frustrated. Growing pot is ruining my relationship; I would rather be poor and happy, sleeping on the bus with no mortgage payment, than living like this. But Michael will not give up, and he's made that perfectly clear to me. I will let the universe decide my fate.*

Plans were laid for the next room—Michael was back on duty and in charge of all things dope-related. I hung up my pot-growing hat and tried to concentrate on things I was good at: vacuuming, cooking, eating, gardening and hanging out with Daisy.

As 1997 approached, Michael grew new mothers for the upcoming outdoor season and honed his skills in hydroponics. The Love Shack now housed two giant tabletop grows, with Michael's signature greed for more pot making it almost impossible to access the plants. In a twelve-by-fourteen-foot room, he built two tables completely together in the middle and spanning move than eight feet across. Both tables touched the wall at one end, making it barely possible to squeeze around one side of them. He actually crawled on his knees on a plank to get to the middle of the tables, risking burning himself on a thousand-watt bulb.

The bulbs were on a slow-moving tracker, providing abundant opportunities for collisions. I avoided the room at all costs. Even at half of Michael's size, I became bitchy and claustrophobic every time I was forced to enter.

One day, when Michael was away, I showed the room to Tony. He had been growing modestly but successfully for almost two years, and I knew I could count on his honesty.

"Okay, why the hell would anyone build a room like this?" I asked, barely able to shove open the door and squeeze in.

After surveying the cramped room full of buckets and supplies piled high to the ceiling and spilling out from under the tables, Tony gave the perfect one-word answer: "Greed."

It is greed that I believe to be the downfall of all growers, and I saw no reason why we shouldn't fail.

YEAR SIX, 1997

Billy's Areas

Michael struggled to support his family—and a lot of down-and-out friends—with his greedy growing style. Although he had a lengthy history of trying to help or employ people who were really beyond it, 1997 began with Michael growing solo. Spring arrived with a clean slate on the horticulture horizon. There would be nothing even resembling a partner this year, although I was sure he could always dig up another broke, unemployed alcoholic to help him plant his crop for less than seventy-five thousand dollars.

Based on a high recommendation from my father, we had hired a reputable logger to selectively clear our overgrown little farm. Of course, he noticed our greenhouse stuffed with marijuana the first day and told us not to worry; he wouldn't breathe a word. He also told us that he rented areas to dope growers for a percentage; and, unlike Ted, he really seemed to know his stuff. Desperately wanting new growing areas and believing the logger to be knowledgeable, Michael considered his offer.

Before entering into any kind of agreement, Michael and the logger went out into the bush together a few times. My parents knew the man well; and he was honest and trustworthy, if not a touch greedy himself. His name was Billy-Bob Washburn. Michael said he had never seen anyone like him in the bush. Five years Michael's senior and maybe five-foot-six, Billy moved like a deer in the forest. The only thing he really stopped for was to put some snuff in his mouth or spit some out at a specific target. While the snuff was being loaded or unloaded, an ever-present ball cap would be removed, revealing a shiny, hairless scalp. As the cap was put back in place after a little head scratch, a sentence comprised mainly of swear words might unravel. But amidst the "cocksuckers" and "bastards" and "dumb cunts" and streams of putrid snuff was a wealth of information. Billy-Bob was a veritable Grizzly Adams.

Michael eventually agreed to try several of Billy's areas. Each area had a spring that appeared in the patch, ran for a few hundred feet and disappeared altogether. All areas had full sun exposure for most of the day and were either so remote no one would want to find them or on a dry hillside miles from water, where no one would suspect them. The elevations of the areas were nearly perfect, and Billy really knew about logging and grazing rights. He had deactivated the road into one of the Ted zones we had used the previous year and had grazing rights for his own cattle in many sectors of Crown Land.

Michael agreed to pay twenty percent of his net to Billy-Bob come harvest. He felt inspired and positive about the coming season, and even I believed in Billy-Bob Washburn. Michael cut a thousand clones.

In late May, an old friend of Michael's phoned, distressed. He was another old guy, new grower, whose whole year had just fallen apart—Mathew Tennor. His paranoid, alcoholic partner had suddenly refused to allow marijuana on the property he and Mathew had been growing on for two years. Mathew did not drink or smoke or do drugs—he had burned himself out years before as a chain-smoking, dope-dealing, dope-smuggling, head-butting party animal. Clean and sober for eleven years, he was intelligent, a fabulous cook, clean, quiet and had money in the bank. We moved Daisy to our bedroom and insisted that Mathew stay with us for the summer.

Mathew arrived in a big red Ford with six or seven hundred clones that were ready to plant. He squeezed out from behind the steering wheel and slowly unfolded his large body. "Well, Hokensons, I made it. I sure appreciate you guys helping me out like this. I can't believe Rick changed his mind like that at the last second. What a shocker. Oh, well, life goes on."

He laughed his signature gale-force chortle and hugged us

simultaneously.

Michael had offered to share some of his new areas with Mathew; I welcomed the company and intelligent conversation. Mathew had cut a holiday short to attend our wedding, and we had only seen him once since. As we unloaded his belongings into the house and greenhouse, we caught up on each other's lives.

An enjoyable routine was soon established. Every morning, we'd all wake up and eat breakfast together in our tiny kitchen. Michael loved to eat; Mathew lived to eat. Then the men would head off to work in separate vehicles, each with a helper, supplies and ATV. I'd stay home with Daisy and work in the garden or prepare food for the men, who were growing in more ways than one. Michael was soon down to one pair of thick brown overalls— everything else was too small to contain his rapidly expanding waistline. Mathew needed a high-calorie intake to maintain his figure, which was Santa-like, only hard instead of jiggly.

Michael enlisted Tony's help—a shock to everyone, including Tony—and Mathew hired Tim. Tony had recently rented a ten-acre farm only minutes from our house, happy to be near his surrogate family again. Tim arrived late most mornings with unbrushed teeth, no work clothes and a giant joint already on the go. Tony arrived on time to the minute every day and went home as clean as a newly scrubbed baby.

Tim quietly asked Mathew one day, "Hey, dude, is that Tony guy some rich kid who lives around here looking for a rush?"

"No," answered Mathew, amused. "Not at all, actually. He's known Mike and Mary-Ann for years. He's just bored and wants to help out."

In casual conversation at work one day Tony had simply told Tim he didn't really need the money, and he was only working for something to do to relieve boredom. By this time, Tony had been growing pot indoors for a few years and was supporting himself quite comfortably. He had a strain called "Big Bud" that seemed to enjoy being covered in whiteflies and watered only once a week. Being financially comfortable at twenty-two was something Tim could not relate to.

The Tony growing philosophy was to do as little as possible. He would do something only if it was necessary for the survival of his room. He watered only when his plants were bone dry, never sprayed any fungicides or pesticides, never gave his crop special growth promoters like thirty-five percent liquid oxygen or CO_2; and despite his lethargic nature, he usually did very well. Every grower we knew now grew hydroponically, but not Tony. He grew in dirt. But it was Tony who always had extra money stashed and was quick to lend it if someone was in need.

Both Tony and Tim were hired strictly for spring start-up to help prepare the new areas for planting. Tim needed every penny to paint his truck black—again—and keep himself supplied with smoke. Tony would use the work to bulk up his thin body and redeem himself in Michael's eyes.

The first area supplied by Billy-Bob was called Grizzly. It was aptly named, as generations of hunters and trappers had seen grizzly bears and their unmistakable signs of inhabitance all over the mountain. The road to Grizzly was long and treacherous, requiring a four-wheel drive as well as an all-terrain vehicle and large *cojones* for the last part of the journey.

After two hours of travel on narrow, pitted old logging roads, a river crossed the trail in front of them, with banks of fifteen feet on both sides. With the trucks hidden miles away, the heavily laden ATVs had to portage the swollen, raging river. Frigid foam sprayed high above the gushing water as it smashed against the huge, smooth stones in the riverbed. Spring runoff and high water coincided with planting time.

Tim and Tony walked across the river on planks placed over various rocks. The two aging growers had to drive their machines across, and this was no easy task. Mathew had a new four-wheel-drive quad and usually made the crossing without too much difficulty. He did weigh over two hundred-fifty pounds and looked absolutely hilarious perched on top of the little blue bike, revving and jerking his way across the water.

Michael, on the other hand, had a tiny two-wheel-drive bike that was over twenty years old. He took many a spill in the freezing water, smashing his bones and losing things off the racks as the water threw him around. He usually got stuck about halfway across, and everyone had to push and pull on his bike as he steered it to the other side.

Once they were out of the river and safely back on the road, the descent to the patch began. Billy-Bob loved this patch and highly recommended it for many reasons, difficult access being its best feature. Police and thieves alike surely wouldn't go to such lengths for a small crop of marijuana. Another feature of this patch was its perfect southern exposure. The area was a vast swamp fed by several springs flanked by a high mountain face to the northwest. The elevation was 2500 feet; but to get to the patch, the road rose to over 5000 feet, a height entirely unsuitable to growing pot. It was only on the far side of the river that the road finally descended.

A forest fire had burned through the swamp in the late 1960s, removing most of the large trees and leaving the patch cleared and open. It also displaced most of the bear population. The government left the entire burn area untouched to study the natural regeneration of a post forest-fire forest. This meant no logging practices or tree planting had occurred in over twenty-five years. Grizzly was like some lost piece of wilderness at the end of the earth.

The worst feature of Grizzly was its bug population. The black flies and mosquitoes were so abundant they were actually one massive, black, slow-moving cloud. When new blood arrived in the swamp, the cloud of hungry insects descended and fed and bit through bug spray and clothing, stopping at nothing to get a piece of the action. Michael wore one hundred-percent DEET, a chemical insect repellant so strong that it actually melted his watchstrap to a plastic-covered bale of dirt during the hike in. The watch had to be cut off his arm, and at this point he vowed to quit using chemicals on his skin. The bugs at Grizzly mocked the DEET, anyway. The best thing to do was cover up and try to forget about them.

When they were not under attack by the dusky, prevailing cloud, there were other hurdles to overcome. The ground at Grizzly was sopping wet all year round. Every step was slow and ankle-deep in putrid muck. It was hard to get around with heavy supplies on your back and fifty-pound pails of fertilizer scraping your legs raw with every squishy step.

Mathew and Michael did manage to prepare four hundred holes by planting time. Michael had three hundred and Mathew only one hundred, as he was experimenting with a new strain.

Tim spent his last day at Grizzly half bent over and virtually useless. Everyone else knelt in the muck beside the holes working frantically, eagerly anticipating the end. When questioned about his lack of performance, Tim earnestly said, "I don't have work pants like you guys, dude. All I've got are my good jeans."

With the toughest patch ready to plant, the crew moved on to Fag Hiker. On a beautiful June morning, the two trucks putted along an abandoned logging road en route to the new area. Two men were seen hiking on a trail near the patch. Mathew, Michael and Tony thought nothing about the hikers, but Tim became nervous and paranoid

"I don't like the looks of those guys, man. I'm sure that they're cops. That one dude is a cop for sure, man, and that other dude looks like a retired cop...or a high school principal."

Mathew said, sarcastically, "I think they're probably just a couple of fags out for a romantic stroll in the woods."

"Why would you think they were cops?" asked Tony. "How can you be so sure?"

"Well, did you see the shoes them guys were wearing?" Tim raised his eyebrows and nodded his head as if he were really on to something.

"No. Well, maybe, but what do shoes have to do with it?" Tony continued to probe.

"Everything," stated a convinced Tim. "The shoes are a dead giveaway, man. Real hikers wear hiking boots or hiking shoes. Them guys just had runners on, and I know they're up to something out here."

Tim continued to believe what his eternally stoned brain told him and was always on the lookout for the "high school principal." Neither Michael nor Mathew were homophobic and meant no disrespect to any of their gay brothers when they named the area Fag Hiker at the end of the day.

The patch was a series of narrow, winding clearings that ran alongside a creek. It was easy to get to and a little close to the road; but after Grizzly, everyone welcomed the chance to work in a friendly area close to home. Michael put three hundred plants in and Mathew one hundred and fifty. Tim's comment about the high school principal became a running joke and was used constantly throughout the year. Mathew said it was worth hiring him just for that.

Fag Hiker was prepped and planted in four days, and the men were ready to move on. The next area to be visited by Mathew and Michael they simply called 2100 Road. The name corresponded with some technical location identification used by Forestry and the logging companies. They had Upper 2100 and Lower 2100, the logging road used for access to both patches running right through the middle. This area was beautiful and easy to work in. The bugs weren't too bad, the walk in was enjoyable and both patches had a spectacular view of lake and mountains. Both growers put in over two hundred plants, and things went smoothly.

Michael did think Mathew left a bit of a trail from the road and repeatedly asked him to take a different route each time, but a guy Mathew's size and age couldn't be too athletic in the bush. His favorite part of the day was always chow time, and he seemed to be getting bigger as the season wore on; so there was quite a trail leading to the start of their upper plot. The first time I was taken there to work I easily found my own way in by following Mathew's bear-sized path.

Lower 2100, however, had a sneaky, overgrown entrance. We entered the lower patch from high above, where the unspoiled, picturesque spring began. This was to facilitate the downhill packing in of heavy supplies; and by our covering so much ground, there was no trail left by the repeated trips into the patch. Michael put his favorite strain in the lower patch and continued to prepare areas.

The next area was called Manson, and it was ugly. I've been to every patch Michael has ever had and hired to work for friends in many others, yet I was never allowed to go to Manson. The patch was named for the creek that fed the area, although I'd initially thought it was some kind of reference to Charles Manson. It might as well have been. Manson Creek had an evil feeling about it. Growing there was insane.

On a bright, sunny day, the four-mile approach to this patch was always dark and gloomy. There were two ways into Manson—by helicopter or straight up the creek on foot. We didn't own a helicopter, so Michael was forced to carry everything up the slippery creek. The only available vegetation to hang on to was devil's club, *oplopanax horridus*, an aptly named plant. It thrives in the underbrush of old-growth timber, sheltered from the sun by giant hemlocks and cedars. The dark-green leaves are broad and rounded, hiding hundreds of long, sharp spines that cover the stalk. Everyone's natural instinct to grab hold of something eventually prevailed, cutting, slicing and scratching the determined growers to shreds.

The first day in Tony took one look at the jagged vertical trail and refused to budge. He told Michael and Mathew they were nuts and the path far too dangerous.

Michael told Tony, "Well, you can fucking well climb that creek or walk home by yourself. Billy and I hiked in three weeks ago and had no problems; we're both twice your age."

Against his will, Tony made the perilous ascent to the patch three times that first day, bringing all the supplies to the edge of the patch. Michael enjoyed this immensely. Halfway up the trail was a huge cedar that had fallen across the creek. It was covered in moss and lichens, shrouded by a canopy of mist from the creek and tall, looming old-growth timber. The only way into the patch was across the creek, the slippery old tree providing the only feasible bridge—at a height of over twenty feet. Miraculously, no one ever fell. Manson was planted in three long days.

This area was one hundred percent guaranteed by Billy-Bob. It was so difficult to access that it had always been thief-proof. No other growers had ever rented the area, for obvious reasons. Billy had put a few plants in at Manson every year for the last ten and always been successful.

"So, Mikey, what do you think of Manson? Nice, eh?" Billy removed his hat and scratched his shiny scalp. "I'll tell you what, any cocksucker crazy enough to go in there—man. Shit, isn't that something? Did you salt in a few big bastards up there?" Billy's false teeth slipped out, and he stopped to replace them, his enthusiasm obvious.

"Yeah, Billy. I put a few in. If I don't die dragging it out and down that fucking hill, we'll make some money at Manson."

Mathew wasn't crazy about the location but did put a few plants in. The hike in left him shaking and short of breath. Michael loved Manson and put in as many plants as he thought the area could hold. After being hit so hard by police and thieves, he dared anyone with enough balls to go in and take his pot

Mathew always thought things through and came up with theories for everything. He had a theory about how Billy-Bob found growing areas and saw no reason for giving a total stranger twenty percent of everything he had, so he proposed that he and Michael find a test area of their own. They looked for days and finally settled on a place that seemed to have all the necessary requirements. Both growers put fifty plants in, gave them lots of slow-release fertilizer and vowed not to check for over a month. If the water supply dried up, the plants would die and the area be written off. If the plants were too wet, they'd probably get stem rot and mold. Only time would tell.

With one hundred plants in, staked and caged, they left for the day, slowly walking over the marshy ground that would lead them back to the truck. Partway back, Mathew heard a soft grunt. He assumed it was Michael and kept on walking. Then, he heard it again and cautiously asked his friend, "Did you hear something, Mike?"

"No. What did it sound like?"

Mathew tried to reproduce the grunt as the sound carried through the trees accompanied by a thunderous splashing and the crackling of bushes. Both tired old friends started running through the swampy grass, tools flying, hats knocked off in the thick brush that surrounded the marsh. They ran all the way back to the truck, with the determined *splash! splash!* noises overpowering the grunting, closing in behind them.

The new area had been tentatively called Bear Shit, for obvious reasons; but it was renamed as they finally spotted the moose they had startled. He galloped through the swamp effortlessly, on legs that seemed ten feet long. As he emerged through the thin tree line he veered away from the truck and continued his boundless pace back into the safety of the forest. He must have been grazing in the swamp as Mathew and Michael quietly worked for hours. Later, a friend of Michael's who was an avid hunter and bush man informed them he'd rather share space with a grizzly than a male moose in rutting season. The area became known as Moose, formerly Bear Shit.

A few miles up the road from Moose was another area of Billy-Bob's. He had drawn Michael a map and described the low-lying swamp as best as he could. Mathew and Michael easily found the place and deemed it suitable for four hundred plants. The patch was very large, probably the biggest area we had. A spring bubbled near the entrance of the patch, eventually feeding into a creek that crossed over onto private land and disappeared into a dense forest. Tim and Tony spent several days working in the gardens near the creek and enjoyed the refreshing water and breezy valley.

Near the end of planting, Tim wandered up the creek one day to relieve himself. He leisurely rolled a joint and drank from the creek before preparing to head back to the others. Only a couple of feet away from where he'd just filled his water bottle was the rotting carcass of a cow. The smell imbedded itself in his nostrils just as he spotted the swollen, maggot-infested lump on the ground beside the creek. Gagging and sputtering, Tim ran all the way back to Michael and Tony, breathlessly describing what he'd just seen.

"A dead cow?" Michael repeated.

"Yeah. And it's pretty gross, dude. I can't believe we've been drinking out of that creek all this time and we're not...infected or anything."

Everyone wandered up the creek and gawked at the dead cow before going home that night. Satisfied that the cow had died of natural causes and the area wasn't *infected*, they named the patch Dead Cow. By the next trip in, the cow had all but disappeared, leaving only a shiny skeleton with ragged bits of skin and flies buzzing around it.

With all of the main areas planted, both Michael and Mathew still had a few clones left. They decided to try another area of their own just down the road from Grizzly. They called it Griz 2. It made sense to plant here because the patch could be serviced on the way to Grizzly. The area was fairly close to the road and required only a short hike through a large swamp and a forest filled with young alder and birch.

With his last plants in the ground, Mathew returned home to pick up his belongings and clear things up with his former partner. He then drove back to our area and looked for a place to rent.

Michael, of course, had a couple of areas without Mathew—his acreage and a vast alpine swamp just discovered by Billy-Bob. Every year since he'd owned it, Michael had successfully grown on his private land. In six years, he'd harvested around four hundred pounds of pot on his property. The first year, a deer had chewed two of his plants, which he thought was cute. Other than that, no person or animal had taken so much as a plant from his unfenced, abandoned land.

Michael or someone else sometimes guarded the property but only sporadically. And guarding never involved anything other than someone's being there. We took this as a sign from our Marijuana God. He wanted us to keep growing and providing good quality pot to all those pot smokers out there, many of whom were chronically ill and relying on it.

The new swamp was a massive flat marsh cupped between several mountaintops. Michael had promised to share this area with a new friend of his—whom I disliked on sight. He was a bodybuilder named Jacob whose neck looked too short for his body, which looked too long for his legs because his muscles were all too big. He was also prettier than all my girlfriends put together.

Jacob always looked as if he'd just come from the beauty salon, which he probably had. Every inch of him was always freshly waxed, coiffed, shaved and tanned. I also thought he was too nice— downright obsequious—and I had a lifelong fear and loathing of bodybuilders.

Jacob's first season of outdoor growing had been highly unsuccessful. He latched on to Michael the previous summer, constantly plaguing him with questions and problems he could have answered himself by purchasing a book. He stared at Michael the way my mother-in-law admires her limited edition Pope plates—the glassy-eyed this-is-my-savior-look. I hated it that this super-positive young kid who had never worked a day in his life or gotten his hands dirty expected Michael to take him in and share his hard-earned knowledge. I secretly hoped something heavy would fall on Jacob's perfect head.

Michael always liked to meet fellow growers and exchange strains and information. Although Jacob had nothing to offer in the way of groundbreaking information, they wanted to grow together somewhere and chose to each do a small patch in this new area referred to as Lost World. Jacob hoped to learn from Michael, although he insisted on using an unproven strain because it was said to have an enormous yield. Michael enjoyed spending time with enthusiastic young people and promised me he would never go into the bush alone. I had no say in the matter anyway.

With Tony and Tim finished for the season and all of the plants in the ground, Michael and Mathew now rode together and shared the burden of maintenance in their rented areas. On a routine trip to Grizzly one day they encountered something that forever changed how they approached growing.

Neither Mathew nor Michael owned a gun; it was something they just never thought about. The two growers worked quietly and quickly about two hundred feet from each other. In every shared area, Michael would take one side of the patch and Mathew the other. They only came together if they were both using the waterhole at the same time or sharing a tool or supplies.

Michael saw it first and said, "What the fuck is that?" as every hair on his body stood on end.

Mathew quietly answered, "That would be a bear."

"What kind of bear would that be?" whispered Michael, but Mathew didn't answer.

It was definitely a bear but it looked odd. Its neck was long and humped and its fur mangy and silvery-brown. It had a very long nose, a lean, awkward body and looked more like a huge dog than a bear. As it spotted the startled men, it stood up on a log and sniffed the air, nose pointed to the heavens. Disturbed, it reared onto its hind legs and dropped, swinging its head from side to side, releasing a torrent of drool from its open mouth.

Most black bears run away when they encounter humans, and pot growers see black bears all the time. This thing was different. Remembering something he'd read, Michael started waving his arms in the air and yelling loudly; but the bear stood its ground. Mathew remained silent and still, probably coming up with a theory of some sort.

"Don't just stand there, Matt! Scream or something!" demanded a shaking Michael. Surging with adrenaline, he picked up a log and thrust it high above his head to give the illusion of hugeness. He shook the log up and down while yelling at the bear, which was still drooling and thrashing its ugly head from side to side. Mathew, by this time, had also started yelling and waving his arms in the air. Continuing to employ their strategy, they slowly started walking towards the trail that would lead them out of the patch.

As Michael and Mathew walked, so did the bear, completely parallel with them and maybe fifty feet away. It only stopped to rear or stare at the petrified trespassers. Their pace quickened to an all-out run, big guts jiggling as trembling legs scrambled to carry them to the safety of the quads on the road.

Once up the last chunk of grassy bank, Michael reached his machine and turned it on, revving the engine and honking the dinky little horn. The bear vanished into the forest. Michael and Mathew caught their breath and reviewed the incident to try and figure out what had just happened.

They agreed to never go to Grizzly again without bear mace, flare guns, rifles and a new device called a *bear banger.* When they'd calmed down, they drove down the mountain and described what they'd seen to Billy-Bob and Brad Martin, a hunting and fishing guide. Both experts came to the same conclusion—Michael and Mathew had encountered a young male grizzly. If that wasn't bad enough, they had probably just planted their crop in his living room.

The grizzly at Grizzly became an ongoing concern. Each trip revealed bags of fertilizer ripped open and eaten. Pack sacks were chewed, coolers and lunch boxes poked with long, sharp teeth and buckets and pots crumpled to nothing. Mathew left a coat accidentally in the patch one night and returned to find it shredded and half-gone. Plants in bags were thrown around and smashed, yet the bear itself was not spotted again. As for the log Michael held above his head in an attempt to intimidate the bear, it was actually so heavy he and Mathew together were not capable of lifting it on a subsequent visit to the patch.

I thought the bear might have died after eating an entire twenty-kilogram bag of slow-release fertilizer, but whenever I went to Grizzly I hired Tony to walk behind me all day with a loaded rifle.

Just my luck, Grizzly became Michael's favorite patch. He insisted on continuing to use the spot—bear or no bear, it was just too good an area to give up. Billy-Bob offered to get a hunting tag for the bear and kill the "son-of-a-bitchin' cocksucker" for us; but Michael felt that we were the ones at fault, trespassing in the bear's territory, and he was right.

Upon entering the patch, the new rule was that the bear be given fair warning. This meant firing a few shots into the air with the rifle and letting off a bear banger. Bear bangers are little pen-shaped devices that shoot out an explosive like a firecracker. The shot goes at least a hundred feet and makes a bang loud enough to scare a drooling grizzly. The other rule was teamwork only, no solo trips to this area or any other.

The devil's club at Manson paled in comparison to the bear at Grizzly, and the season progressed without much further excitement. I went to work more this year than any other because Daisy was now walking, talking and toilet-trained. She enjoyed staying with her grandparents at the lake, and I could stand being away from her for a night or two.

My favorite area to visit soon became Grizzly because I loved the long ride in on the quads. The access road was full of life and boasted an incredible lake view. Grouse would run out in front of us as the quads approached, leading their fuzzy babies down the road in a panicky but adorable parade.

The changes in flora and fauna were what most impressed me.

The leaves turned color from green to startling oranges and reds; rabbits, coyotes, squirrels and birds filled the mountain with life; lupines and Queen Anne's lace dotted the banks that had recently been vibrant with Indian paintbrushes and arnica; dragonflies took the place of butterflies and there was always something sweet to eat.

In June we nibbled wild strawberries; in August I'd squat amongst the multitude of blueberry bushes and eat until someone yelled at me to work. There were old apple trees at the bottom of the road and Saskatoon bushes all the way up. Aside from my intense fear of the slobbering young grizzly, I found it to be a complete paradise. After the long, cool ride up, we'd work in the patch, completely covered to keep the bugs out, in what always seemed to be unbearable heat. On the way out after work, we'd stop at the river and dunk ourselves and fill our water bottles with the icy, clean mountain water. Nothing had ever made me feel more alive than a trip to Grizzly.

* * *

AUGUST 1—*I'm really enjoying working with the guys on maintenance trips to the new areas. Other than Manson, where I am forbidden to go, I've become part of the crew; I even went to work in Michael's place a few times! I feel incredibly strong. I believe that I'm becoming a capable grower and eagerly anticipate our trips into the bush.*

It's recently hit me that we now calmly rely on marijuana as our main source of income; all of our time and efforts are invested solely in the growing of our favorite herb. It's been ages since I've dreamed of the helicopter or being arrested, so I guess I'm o.k. with it all. We don't have time to fight about it right now, anyway—we owe a lot of money and even I can't imagine any other way to pay so much back.

The long summer days stretched into weeks and all of the areas were untouched and flourishing as fall approached. The three of us crammed into Mathew's Ford, headed for 2100 Road. Waves of heat spilled from the sky and baked the parched earth under the tires. The slow-moving truck filled with dust, choking and blinding us as Mathew bellowed with laughter.

"I'm glad you find this amusing, Mathew," I grumbled, "but could you pick up the pace a bit and let me get the hell out of the truck?"

After what seemed an interminable amount of time, we reached the pull-off. Michael helped me out of the truck and loaded my little packsack with supplies. I ran ahead of the men, who carried far more weight than I, and was first to find the upper patch crisscrossed in string. So much string was tangled and swaying throughout the patch that the name of the area was forever after known as String; Upper and Lower.

This was a devastating discovery; the plants were monstrous shrubs and completely surrounded by the thread that usually signifies the end of a patch. Whoever tied the string would probably harvest the crop prematurely, and there was nothing we could do about it.

As predicted by Michael, the next visit to Upper String was a sad one. All of our plants had been stolen. Mathew's strain was later than ours and just barely into bud, making it undesirable to the thieves. Upon closer inspection of Mathew's patch, we noticed some of his plants had been chewed. Not dainty chewing but voracious gnawing and devouring. A lot of the plants were dying as a result of weakened stems. They had been attacked from ground level to two feet up and peeled all the way around, causing many of the large, heavy tops to lean over, eventually splitting the plants in half. This was almost as sad as Michael's empty holes, the short, stubby stalks left to remind us of the fertile giants that had inhabited the ground all summer. Mathew promised himself he would return and cage his remaining plants in an attempt to salvage the area. He never did.

I wondered aloud just what kind of asshole would steal someone's entire crop. To take everything, none of which was theirs to begin with, and leave the poor sod who planted it and babied it all year *nothing*. Not even enough to roll a joint. Not enough to recoup your investment. Who were these assholes, and where did they live? I wanted to catch one and tie him up and beat him with a rubber chicken.

I begged Mathew to booby trap his remaining patch, certain the unknown assholes would return for more. Mathew mumbled something about shotgun shells and fishing line, and he said he'd think about it. He thought about it too long and didn't do a damn thing. The next trip to String was predictably light; there was no dope to pack out—the only pot there was the chewed and rotten remains of Mathew's uppermost plot. Mathew and Michael abandoned Upper String, vowing to never grow there again.

Lower String was thriving and completely untouched. We made trips in only when necessary, as Michael was sure the beaten-down path leading into Upper String had led to its demise. His first trip yielded ten pounds while Mathew checked his plants, waiting for his strain to fill out. Mathew was far more patient than either Michael or I, and we counted our blessings.

The first pot to come off usually sold quicker and for more money, as the market was in favor of the grower. By October, the market was usually flooded with thousands of pounds of outdoor pot and only beautiful, high-quality produce sold. Pot that was wet, of poor quality or not esthetically pleasing would be passed over and rejected. Buyers could pick and choose, and many growers couldn't give their stuff away.

With the harvest underway and things looking promising, we discussed the building of a new house. Building a house was something we'd always talked about; and we both knew that, eventually, we would outgrow the little farmhouse we were living in. Five hundred square feet wasn't much space for three people, revolving part-time houseguests, four cats and tons of junk and antique furniture. We agreed to save our old house, use what we could from it and build a new house adjoining the old.

Michael had just received $100,000 from the sale of his half of the property he and Jimmy had owned. It had been one of the most difficult transactions he had ever made. As the sole owner of the development property on paper, Jimmy was able to take out a $65,000 mortgage when he got short of money. He'd quit his job after the fall harvest of '93 and become a fulltime drunk. He had been using our money to show the bank how much equity he had in "his" land, enabling him to borrow against the property. This clandestine mortgage would be the downfall of Michael and Jimmy's relationship.

Angry and shocked, after weeks of trying we finally located Jimmy and confronted him. When we asked what the hell he had been thinking, it became apparent he honestly believed the land was his.

"I know what's going on," Jimmy slurred. "I know all about your little father-in-law/son-in-law conspiracy. Well, you're not screwing old Jimmy over. You want this fucking land, just try to come and take it!" he ranted.

Years of excessive drinking had made him delusional and paranoid. He actually thought we were out to get him and take away "his" land. The battle over what to do with the property went on for two years. Jimmy refused to sell us his half and said if he had anything to do with it the land would remain untouched and in his name for as long as he was alive. In other words, we had spent about eighty thousand dollars and had nothing to show for it.

Jimmy disappeared. Michael hired a lawyer and a private investigator to track him down and force him to dissolve their partnership. The land went up for bid, and Jimmy bought Michael out with funding from his mother, who had co-signed for his first mortgage and technically already owned the land, and his old boss from up north. Michael came out on top, recouping his initial investment and making a decent profit. This drove the wedge between the once-inseparable cousins even deeper.

With his dreams of a future in land development shattered, Michael forged ahead as a fulltime grower. Jimmy insisted he was the victim of a conspiracy and forged ahead as a fulltime alcoholic. Secretly, I still loved Jimmy and would have forgiven him in a second; but Michael was deeply hurt and humiliated. The cousins would never speak again.

Michael wanted to use the proceeds of the sale as investment money, but I convinced him now was the time to build a house. I figured that if we waited until we had all the money we'd be putting around in electric wheelchairs with no teeth eating strained prunes.

By then, I wouldn't want a new house.

Michael always wanted to say yes to my every wish and make me happy, so he finally gave in. We decided to get as far as we could with the cash we had and then use pot money from the fall harvest to finish. We looked for a place to rent and started packing at the end of August.

* * *

SEPTEMBER 6—*Our rental house is a small, hideous, spider-infested piece of shit that should actually be condemned. Of course, we know we'll have marijuana in the house in one form or another, so we can never complain about anything. The rent is cheap, and the house is on a small acreage with virtually no neighbors; in that respect, it's perfect. Perfect in the Pot World is very different from perfect in the normal world.*

The ad in the paper said "three-bedroom house." What they meant was one bedroom and two concrete cellars with no heat or windows and plenty of spiders and packrats in the walls. Daisy is permanently camped in our bedroom, as the house has only one room suitable for sleeping in. The tiles in the bathroom have all lifted to expose an old plywood floor smeared with years of mildew and grime. My two beautiful cats were riddled with fleas inside the first week, and a flea hopped off Daisy's head at the dinner table one night and disappeared into the air.

I spent the first few weeks in our new home cleaning, sterilizing, painting, fumigating, shampooing and fixing. We moved our own appliances into the house, as the ones provided were unsafe and so grease-caked I refused to use them.

At this point, the really bad stuff hadn't shown up yet. Most of the problems plaguing this house were associated with winter.

Things at our farm were coming along slowly but according to plan. We had hired an architectural salvage company—this meant we'd found a builder who would build us an old-looking house that incorporated salvaged materials. Used wood, fixtures and hardware were a fraction of the price of new and had the authentic look Michael and I both longed for. Our house would look like a one hundred-year-old Victorian farmhouse, only it would be brand new.

The builder had been salvaging heritage buildings in the area for years and dreamed of meeting a nice couple like us. He was an eccentric Russian fellow named Stan Swidlikoff. Stan was forty-seven years old and built like an Olympic athlete. He was a health food nut who didn't drink or smoke. He did have one weird little habit, though; he was a pathological liar. The lies he told were harmless and silly because they were so obvious; and we discussed them at great length. Both Michael and I felt that as long as he showed up for work and built the house he could have his delusional fantasies about dinosaur bones and his past life as a great modern artist. We felt fortunate to have met Stan and couldn't wait to watch our new house take shape.

In today's market, most contractors build houses with vinyl siding, white plastic doors with fake stained glass and those multi-light panels in the bathroom. We wanted wooden siding, antique doors, real stained glass, wainscoting, wraparound porches and, of course, a turret. We also wanted to save money and save trees. Not everyone was as enthused about working with old stuff as we were, and Stan was actually brilliant. He knew more about the Victorian era than anyone we'd ever met. He was incredibly artistic and passionate, and we felt that he was capable of building our dream house. We forged ahead and gave Stan everything he needed to get started.

September was a tough month for the building crew, as it rained almost every day. It was also a bad month for our ripening pot. By October, Michael had lost almost fifty pounds to mold. Every day, he regretted letting me talk him into building a house that he was not ready to build. Our pile of money was slipping away, and we were trapped in this limbo between homes. Stopping what we had started seemed impossible, so we crossed our fingers and prayed to our Pot God.

Stan was saving our old house and attaching it to the foundation of the new one. It took seven days to jack up the old house and get it in position to move. Just as everything would be getting close to ready, the house would sink in the mud and have to be elevated and re-leveled. The crew was cold and soggy as they trudged around in the mud under the tired old house. In retrospect, we probably lost money trying to save the frame of the tiny, stripped-down home, which had been built in 1927.

Most of our initial one hundred thousand dollars had been spent by October first; and all we had to show for it was a foundation, a septic field and a pile of used lumber in our neighbor's field. The old house stood bare and empty, with no siding or windows or doors. The yard was strewn with crumpled tin, chunks of wood, old newspaper insulation and huge piles of mud and rock. The lawn and garden that I'd slaved over for two seasons had been ripped into huge clumps of sod. I referred to it all as the hundred-thousand-dollar hole.

And our financial hole was getting deeper. I felt as if we were sinking in a giant pool of quicksand surrounded by marijuana plants that weren't close enough to grab hold of.

Michael had had bad years before, but there had never been anything like the destruction of mold. It was one thing to have plants stolen or cut down by the police or gnawed on by cute, furry animals; but to watch your crop turn to mush before your eyes was a new form of devastation. The mold spread like wildfire. The cold rain came day after day, making it impossible to salvage most of the sodden, gray crop. We hired two crews to work in two separate houses with a quality control mold inspector.

This job went to Tim's girlfriend, Julie. Tiny, agile and quick, Julie spent her days examining all the pot that everyone had clipped looking for little chunks of mold. She would carefully remove the offending furry spores and keep track of which clippers needed to be more careful. Wages were costing Michael over fifteen hundred dollars per day. Huge bags of moldy pot had to be thrown out daily, only to be replaced by fresh ones. A short month earlier we had money in the bank, and the year was looking promising. How could these pot-growing calamities keep devouring us?

Thieves hit Fag Hiker in early October. We wondered if the pot was taken by the "high school principal" wearing the telltale shoes. Mathew lost almost everything, and Michael lost a good fifteen pounds. Manson and Grizzly were untouched by humans, but Mother Nature swept through both areas in a mold-laden flurry. Griz 2 was completely ripped off, leaving only Moose and Lower String. Both of these patches were salvaged, but neither was a huge producer.

Dead Cow had no mold, but Mathew's late strain was in cold shock. The low-lying valley was loaded with frost every morning, and there was not enough bud on the immature pot to protect it from the cold. Michael harvested most of his plants, although they had turned purple from the cold nights and weren't optimum.

But the real disappointment for Michael was his own property. He had hired a friend of Mathew's to guard it starting the first of September, figuring his golden growing zone would pull us through a tough year. How could we have been so wrong?

The guard was a fifty-year-old alcoholic named Boomer. He was a really nice guy and desperately in need of money. Like all the other guards Michael had hired, he had some problems. Michael swore that all Boomer needed was a break, a chance to make some cash and clear up his debts. I agreed to give him a try. After only a few days, it became clear that alcoholism wasn't the biggest problem; it was the prescription drugs he mixed with it that were the real hazard.

Boomer was an animal lover and showed up with two huge, formerly abused dogs that would kill for him. This was great for Boomer as well as the dogs and us. We had the added security of two intimidating guard dogs, and Boomer had company and protection. The dogs were thrilled to be in the country, running and sniffing and exploring endlessly.

But when Boomer got high on Zanax he called the dogs into the bus with him, and all three slept like babies while someone snuck onto the property and ripped off Michael's best patch.

We drove over to check on him one morning and found him

sleeping in the bus. Both of the dogs were inside and made no noise as we approached. Michael rousted Boomer, who swore he'd been up and checked the plants during the night. We all walked up the hill together to find most of the patches intact, but the best one had been topped.

Topping is a nasty form of thievery. All of the colas are cut off the plant, taking only the biggest and the best buds. The little fluffy branches, containing far less resin and actual dope, are left behind. Michael figured he lost ten or twelve pounds while his "guard" slept peacefully in the bus.

Usually, something like this would not have been catastrophic, but this year it was. Why did we have to get ripped off when we really needed every last plant? Boomer was apologetic and extremely upset and promised to stay awake at night and keep the dogs outside. He and Michael mapped out a strategy and agreed to adhere to it. This lasted for a few days, until Boomer went on a binge and left the property completely unattended.

Boomer had a girlfriend who was addicted to painkillers and also happened to have a ton of money from an insurance settlement she'd just received. When the two of them got together for a night of boozing and pill-popping debauchery, it usually ended with someone in jail or the hospital.

Michael went to harvest one of the patches on the property two days after the theft to find the place abandoned. If Boomer didn't have a rock-solid alibi, like death or imprisonment, he was going to be fired. Michael left a note on the door of the bus explaining to Boomer why he wasn't working out as a guard. Two days later, we got a note on the door of our house that read "Back on Duty!! Sorry, Chief. P. S. I'm not fired. Love Boomer." He drove home from a two-day binge on Xanax and vodka and went right back to work like nothing had happened. Michael let him stay.

The stress about the new house reached an all-time high, and Michael and I argued every day. Stan had spent so much money in the first two months, and he constantly needed more. That was the nature of building a house; we just didn't know it yet.

With the outdoor year coming in short of the mark and the new house sucking up money like a vacuum cleaner, we turned the basement of our rental home into a giant grow room. Michael calculated what he thought we'd need to live on through the coming year and then added what Stan should need to finish the house. If we grew indoors all winter, everything should be fine.

We did make a trip to Stan's storage barn and felt much better after seeing acres of stuff he'd bought for our house. By now, he knew we grew pot and lots of it. This was totally okay with him. He understood he might have to wait for money at times or be laid off until a room came down.

I can't honestly say when everything started to fall apart with Stan. His stories of dinosaur bones under his trailer and his multiple degrees in parapsychology started to bother me. It wasn't just that Indiana Stan was building our home; it was the obvious lies he was now trying to feed us that directly related to the house.

Michael spent a few days trying to figure out just where we stood with Stan and came to the conclusion we were basically married to him for the duration. He was so deep into us financially, and we needed our hole turned into a viable house; so Michael thought it best that we try to weather the storm. This was a test of our patience and endurance.

By now, the rental house had turned into a wet, moldy shit hole with rotting drywall covered in black mold. The front door sported a greenish-gray fuzzy mold I finally had to complain about. Daisy and I had both developed chest infections that were surely caused by our literally dripping walls and windows. As fast as I cleaned and bleached the ceilings and walls in most of the house the mold would reappear. The multitude of plants in the basement gave off volumes of moisture caused by transpiration. This only added fuel to the fire in a house that was poorly insulated and had no ventilation. The moist air was trapped within the rat-infested walls, creating a perfect environment for my favorite fungus. Finally, we bought a dehumidifier and left most of the windows open all day long. This alleviated some of the problem and made for a hefty heating bill.

The house was still cold and full of spiders, and when we lay in bed at night the unidentified four-legged vermin scurried about endlessly behind the wallboard. I had taken to pounding on the offending wall or ceiling with a broomstick. What had become of my life? I felt like a crack mother raising her only offspring in a fleabag derelict tenement infested with pneumonia-causing mold and vampire bats.

At least the Pot World didn't wholly consume us; the construction of our house provided a new outlet for stress and worry. The only up side to our dwelling was that it was temporary; another month or two and, surely, we'd be in our new house.

The pot year had been pathetic. When all the dust and mold finally settled, Michael had pulled off his worst year, again. What started out as an easy one hundred-fifty pounds came in just light of forty-five. It cost eight hundred dollars per pound to clean the pot, and Billy-Bob got twenty percent of the net in all of his areas. This left us with very little money, somewhere around thirty-five thousand dollars. The ongoing battle over the ill-timed building of *my* house heated up.

YEAR SEVEN, 1998

The Money Pit

Michael and I fought like we'd never fought before. We screamed at each other, insulted each other; and we both threatened divorce. Michael hated the new house with an indelible passion. He had enough sense, however, to know that it had to be finished, and this would require more money—a lot more money.

The grow room in our basement wasn't making enough, so he lit up the Love Shack. The price of indoor pot had dramatically dropped from $3,200 to $2,200 per pound, and the market in B.C. was saturated. The media reported an estimate of one in every seven houses' containing a marijuana grow operation in beautiful British Columbia.

Everyone on the house building crew smoked pot and thought nothing of working beside an outbuilding full of it. If anything happened to go wrong, they'd all plead ignorance. We had to drive to the house every day to feed and water our animals, anyway, so why not have another grow room going?

So, Michael spent all winter doing the one thing he hated more than anything—growing pot indoors. This didn't stop him from working a huge hidden grow room into the house plans. It had been so long since I'd lived in a house without the humming drone of a grow room; at least this one would be hidden and soundproof.

The room was subterranean and would be designed especially to grow pot. The old house sat next to the new one and served as a garage and side entrance. The floor of the garage was partly over the

131

hidden room, which had only one small trapdoor leading into it. Once through the trapdoor, you had to crawl down a narrow ladder that led to a corner of the room. The trapdoor was inside part of the old house and hidden under the floor.

Only two crew members and Michael and I knew about the hidden room. Until the bunker was operational, Michael continued to grow in our rental house and in the Love Shack, generating enough income to continue building.

We drove into the yard one morning and surveyed the crew at work.

"Why does everyone Stan hires have to look like a convict?" Michael wondered aloud.

When you're trying to save money and you're engaged in something illegal, your options in life are somewhat limited. One of Stan's right-hand men was Kerry, a tall, shaky, alcoholic electrician. It took Kerry over a month to wire our house, which would later require three more electricians to finish and fix the job he started. I began asking Indiana Stan questions about things like this, which pissed him off to no end. I was supposed to blindly hand over huge fistfuls of cash without ever questioning his manly abilities to hire people and build houses.

Kerry was a chain-smoking bundle of nerves who never washed his hair or clothes. When not wiring, he doubled as the world's worst carpenter. He put reams of siding on backwards and would often just stop altogether when he got to something he couldn't figure out. This left gaps and holes all over the place that someone else eventually had to redo. The people in charge of redoing Kerry's handiwork weren't much better than he was; only one person on Stan's crew stood out as capable and skilled.

The one girl on the crew, named Henrietta Bond, outshone everyone. Henry was really a man trapped in a woman's body. She worked like a man, she talked like a man, she looked like a man and she was married to a woman. Henry lit her first joint of the day with her morning coffee and puffed away all day long. Somehow, this constant consumption of pot never interfered with her ability to work.

Stan had fired several laborers during the first few months of building but had nothing but praise for Henrietta. She was part of the crew that had disassembled the old house on day one, and she'd worked every day since.

Henrietta impressed us as we slowly got to know her. She had supported her wife and a child from her wife's first marriage for thirteen years. She rarely missed a day of work, and she kept her head down and her mouth shut. It was too bad more of Stan's crew weren't like Henrietta.

The house, by this time, was starting to look less than majestic and Victorian. It looked like the general contractor maybe didn't know what he was doing, or he was running out of money. We had a meeting with Stan to re-evaluate the situation. We decided to give everyone a break for one month. This would give us time to harvest another room, and everyone could relax mentally.

* * *

FEBRUARY 1—*Stan started back to work today, and things seemed a lot more controlled. Michael will oversee all of Stan's expenditures; he'll pay wages and bills and Stan has been reduced to an employee. We borrowed $50,000 against Michael's property to finish the house, and we have to know where every penny is going. The changes have made Stan furious, but it has become obvious to Michael and I that old Stan is in way over his head. Stan is hard-working and a great carpenter but that seems to be about it. He lacks expertise in things like plumbing, wiring and listening.*

Henrietta finally broke down and told us that Stan had developed a gambling problem partway into the project. We'd give him money to buy something for the house or pay wages, and he would drive to the nearest town and bet it all on the horses. At least we finally knew where all the money had been going and why such cheap labor was necessary. That's when things got really ugly.

133

Michael and I showed up at the house one morning to pay wages. We went into the basement where the crew had set up their lunchroom; and there, in the ceiling, was the downfall of Indiana Stan. He had taken miles of old, used ducting and taped it together—it ran uphill and around corners and downhill and—oh, my God, this was to be our heating system! This bunch of rusty, old salvaged garbage held together with duct tape was supposed to carry heat from the huge, brand-new furnace to every room in the house.

I had also given Stan $10,000 the previous week with the understanding that he would fulfill one request—a concrete floor in the basement. He spent every penny and gave me some line about no cement companies being available to pour concrete that week. I phoned around and learned that for about $1,000 any of four or five reputable local companies would have been happy to come out and pour a basement floor for us.

But the ducting was the final straw. Michael told him to get the mishmash of used, fucking garbage the hell out of the house. Stan just argued and tried to lie his way out of it. All of our pent-up emotions and anger over being lied to for months boiled to the surface like bubbling lava and exploded. Michael put his face directly in Stan's and screamed at him at top volume.

"We know about your little gambling problem, Stan, and we hired structural experts to evaluate the house this weekend. They told us to fire you! They told us that you've all but destroyed this house. My God, man! Admit that you're in way over your head!"

Michael also told Stan not to expect any more money. We had a structural engineer coming who estimated another $50,000 would be needed to fix the multitude of problems Stan had created.

At this, Stan all but started crying. He admitted he hadn't paid his rent in two months, and he owed money all over the place. Not believing for a moment that the house he was building could be any less than perfect, he begged to keep his job. He promised to remove the ducting if only he could have another chance...and $10,000 cash. That's when I could take no more. I charged over to where the two men stood under the peeling duct tape and exploded.

"Listen, you stupid moron! We all know you're a pathological liar.

Do you really think anyone believes your stupid fucking dinosaur stories? Why don't you sell the bones under your trailer and pay off some of your bills? And do you think we really believe that you have all these degrees? I think you were in a fucking nuthouse as a patient, and you picked up some of the lingo. And what about this fucking ducting? How dare you put that crap in our house, you lying piece of shit.

"And the concrete I asked you for, that was a lie. I phoned around and checked and you wasted ten thousand dollars and still no concrete. What good are you to us if you won't listen? It's *not* your house, Stan, it's ours. And how come if you're so brilliant you live in a fucking rented trailer that you can't even pay rent on? You're a lying, sneaking idiot! You better get your shit packed up and get the hell out of our house!"

I was vibrating; it felt great. The volcano had erupted and was pouring out all around us for all to see. To finally tell someone who had lied to me for months what I really thought of him—what a relief! If there's one thing I can't stand, it's being lied to.

The entire crew stayed behind as Stan and Kerry packed up and left. Stan stared at the ground and sheepishly told us we were the nicest people he'd ever worked for. Translation—we were the biggest suckers with the deepest pockets he'd ever had the pleasure of hosing.

We all pitched in and worked until the $50,000 ran out—which wasn't very long. The house sat empty and abandoned in the dirty snow, waiting for us to come back and finish her. Stan packed his belongings, had an unsuccessful auction at the farm he'd been renting and left the province. Rumor has it he headed for Saskatchewan to look for dinosaur bones.

* * *

MARCH 16—*We are struggling, treading water, barely able to hold it all together. Still in the rental house, we have two phone bills, two mortgages, two power bills, one rent bill, one car payment; and it's almost spring start-up. That means a huge bill for supplies and wages; I don't know where it's going to come from. And people that Stan neglected to pay keep finding us and giving us bills. We've already paid them, but Stan spent the money and we have to dish it out again. I feel sick all the time, and I'm losing weight again.*

I remember being little and afraid to go to school in the morning. Other kids picked on me for being smart and having a schoolteacher for a mother; I dreaded every day at the tiny elementary school on Pine Street. Mom would squat down, put her hands on my shoulders, look squarely into my eyes and say, "You must be brave, do you understand?" shaking me ever so lightly.

This was what her older sister Bernice would tell her young sibling, a motherless little girl heading off to school from a two-room shack in Northern Alberta. For some reason, the faux seriousness of the ritual always made my mother laugh. I tried to picture Mom grabbing my shoulders and shaking me into forced bravery—I felt no stronger.

The ongoing battle over the house prevailed and strained our new marriage to its limits. I was happy when Michael's days were once again filled with cloning and dreams of next year.

Mathew was working alone this year, and Michael hired Henrietta. The three would meet in the yard of our rental property, which was on the way to all of the growing areas. The main focus this year was Grizzly, with Lower String and Dead Cow as backup.

I convinced Michael to let me grow on our farm. He was hesitant at first but helped me camouflage the patch, and we both felt pretty safe. Because Daisy required my constant attention, I could only work part-time in the bush. I was at the farm every day rebuilding my yard and garden, so it made sense to me to have a small plot of my own there.

I put one hundred holes in and filled them with compost and manure. Michael had rented his property to Jacob and his little brother, disillusioned after a year of mold and theft. My little garden would contain our only pot on private land.

I immediately became paranoid about planting one hundred plants, so I dropped the number to eighty. The holes were far apart and partly hidden by huge birch and cedar trees, and I felt comfortable with my patch.

Every third morning I ran the garden hose from our house as far as it would go and then added several more lengths until I had reached the edge of my patch. Here, underneath a tree, I filled my buckets with water and fertilizer and ran throughout the garden. It took me just over an hour to feed all the plants. Once a week, Michael mixed up a smelly sprayer full of Rocket Fuel, and the plants were given a treat.

Fungicide had been added to our maintenance routine starting the first week of August, as we were determined to never let mold devour a crop of ours again. I carefully tied all of my plants down several times throughout the year and laughed to myself when helicopters flew over. I promised myself and anyone else who would listen that if I were ever busted in my patch I would remove all of my clothes and go naked and silent to jail. I don't know why I wanted to do this; I just promised myself that I would.

By July of 1998 we were firmly in the grip of a drought. The ground was dry and dusty, gardens shriveled up and died and parched animals came into populated areas to drink. In the Pot World, there was an extreme, death-causing occurance sweeping through the forest like a plague. The stalks of plants were chewed near the ground, causing death or weakness to thousands of young marijuana plants. Every grower we knew was experiencing the same destructive phenomenon as we were in most of our areas.

We guessed the chewers must be rabbits or deer and set out to repel them. Someone told us to put chunks of soap around all of our plants because the smell would repulse the critters. This seemed a cheap and harmless solution worth trying. Mathew spent two hundred dollars on Irish Spring soap, the strongest and most repulsive-smelling he could find. Then he and I spent hours sitting on the tailgate of his truck cutting the soap into thimble-sized pieces.

Michael headed to the farm and garden supply store and asked for advice on how to "nicely" get rid of deer. The store manager suggested wolf urine. It was very expensive and something you definitely didn't want to spill on yourself, but a wolf's scent was sure to scare off rabbits and deer. We headed out at five in the morning to hit all the areas in one day and put an end to the crippling chewing. We had lost hundreds of plants by this time and were feeling desperate.

It was my job to distribute the Irish Spring. Mathew filled a pack sack with the green chunks, and I ran from plant to plant, delivering hundreds of strategically placed slivers of stinky soap. Mathew had ripped one of his old housecoats into strips, and he wandered through the bush hanging the strips of cloth in trees. He then dabbed a pungent drop of wolf piss onto each piece of cloth and hoped for the best. Michael splinted hundreds of our plants after applying a vitamin-infused Vaseline-like substance in hopes of saving a few.

A few days later we returned to all of the areas to find the ground littered with more dead plants. Nothing else seemed to be under attack like our pot. Hundreds of new plants had been lost in spite of our sensory assault on the critters. We needed expert advice.

Billy-Bob was consulted. He told us, "I figure its mice, Mikey. Them little bastards will chew anything. She's so fuckin' dry out there this year, every little son of a bitch in the forest'll be after your plants. Fuck."

The juicy marijuana plants were the only things in the parched forests getting an adequate supply of water.

"Now, Mikey, if you want to stop them bastards, a guy should take and cover them stalks so the little pricks can't get at them. Some kind of wire or screen; that'll stop the cocksuckers from chewing on your plants and they'll have to chew on something else."

Billy splattered a dollop of snuff on the ground and shook his head reassuringly.

On the advice of Billy, Michael and I bought miles of window screen and cut it into little one-foot squares. Snugly placed screens, with mesh so small that bugs couldn't penetrate them, were the final answer for Michael and me. We covered the bottom twelve inches of each stem on each living plant tightly with a screen bound by twist ties at the top and bottom and never lost another plant.

Mathew had a theory about the chewing as he sauntered around his plants, misting them with some kind of pepper spray. He had it figured that rabbits, deer or rodents were responsible for the devastation of our plants. Pepper spray was easy to carry, easy to apply and his whole patch was covered in the time it took us to apply four or five screens. The company selling the pepper spray guaranteed to repel all offending animals if the spray was applied correctly and reapplied after wet weather.

The only hurdle left was the utter lack of water and what to do about it. Lower String was all but out of water by August. We usually let Mother Nature water our plants all year and only used water jugs to deliver extra fertilizers or to mix something water-soluble. Michael was ill, and Mathew and I had gone to check on the screens and spray Mathew's plants.

The garden looked thirsty. The spring was still bubbling gently out of the ground, but the creek it fed had dried up. Thistles lined the banks of the patch; their annoying down stuck to everything. The marijuana plants were now half the size of the thistles, fighting for sunlight and water with the prickly giants.

I dropped to my knees in the soft muck and weeded until my hands bled and our plants were no longer shaded. Meanwhile, Mathew had lunch and napped under a tall birch tree. Neither of us had thought to bring a watering jug, and for some reason there were none stashed in the bush. I had no idea when Michael or I would next visit this patch, and it desperately needed water. I looked for a suitable container and found nothing. Then, I had a brainstorm.

I had a plastic bag we had used for the soap chunks in the bottom of my packsack. In the Pot World, we referred to bags this size as *pound bags* because we used them for selling one-pound lots of pot. The bag was actually an extra-large freezer bag. I filled the pound bag in the tiny puddle created by the spring and ran throughout the patch from plant to plant, back to the puddle and so on.

Mathew looked up from under his tree, a small bit of sandwich lodged on his chin and asked, "Are you going to do all your plants like that?"

"Absolutely." I informed him. "I'm going to go until the bag breaks or I get heatstroke. Do you want me to do any of yours?"

"No. I'm thinking they're probably okay," Mathew assured me. "The water table is a lot lower down than you think, and the roots should be getting plenty of water. I'm going to wait it out this time and see how they do."

Translation: I weigh two hundred-sixty pounds, I'm almost fifty years old and my indoor rooms are doing great. Why should I run around in the baking sun with a Baggie full of water when I can just go back to sleep until it's time to go?

Mathew did say something about how I could tell my grandchildren that when I was young times were so tough we had to water our pot plants with a bag.

I was so proud of myself. I ran over logs and through brambles with the ripping plastic bag full of water. Partway through, the bag lost its top and became a half-pound bag; but every thirsty little plant we had received a drink.

I continued running until the bag disintegrated. I threw up from the heat and physical exertion, my head pounding relentlessly; but I felt great. We jumped into Mathew's truck and headed for Dead Cow.

The summer progressed with no change in the weather. Things at Michael's property were in sad shape, and Jacob was the laziest pot grower we'd ever seen. Because he was always jacked up on steroids, I'd expected him to be a powerhouse of energy and productivity. He was actually one of the mellowest people we'd ever met. Jacob was never in a hurry, and he didn't succumb to stress. This spelled disaster for his struggling marijuana plants.

The water system at Michael's property was capable of great things when running properly. A few times each season the screen in the reservoir needed cleaning; and sometimes, the lines could plug up with silt or sticks and, once, a dead rodent. It was a hell of a hike to the reservoir but well worth the effort. Seven or eight hundred plants could easily be watered in one day if the system was running at capacity.

Jacob and his brother, John, had only four hundred plants, and yet it took them all week to give the plants one small drink. Jacob knew that with one day's work he could have enough water pressure to peel paint off a car. He instead chose to sit idly for a five-minute wait as each bucket filled.

Michael couldn't believe his eyes the first time he saw his property. He had leased the acreage to Jacob and provided him with clones and holes for fifty percent of the crop. He told Jacob to hike up to the reservoir, clean it out and to check the water lines to increase the pressure. To this day, Michael has no idea why this was never done—sheer, unadulterated laziness. The tiny clones were always drooping, thirsty and on the brink of death. They never had a chance.

But every week, Jacob and John drove to the bush and sat beside the trickling hose for hours, wondering why their plants were so small. We all prayed for rain; Jacob prayed for a miracle.

Things were not going well at all this year. Again. Mice had conservatively chewed four to five hundred of our plants to death. The cycle of running from patch to patch trying to water everything was exhausting. Most summers, we at least had the odd day off to swim with Daisy or go boating or work around the farm.

Michael was still growing indoors and doing a mighty poor job of it, along with the interminable maintenance schedule for the outdoor crop. We rarely saw each other; and when we did, we argued about the house or growing pot. I felt as though I couldn't take much more. Every year it was the same thing—everything would be looking great; and then, after months of working and hoping and no income— boom!—a disaster.

I couldn't take them like Michael could. He was just so happy to be working for himself and entirely away from people that he really didn't mind any of the setbacks growing pot had to offer. He simply saw growing pot as his small business. He was the boss and CEO, I his only fulltime employee and treasurer. The yearly expenses were his overhead and what was left, his profit. He paid income tax and provided a few part time jobs to unemployed alcoholics throughout the year. Drought, rodents, bears, thieves, cops, mold, frost and any and all other unforeseen accidents were pesky little hurdles that all small businesses experienced.

Michael was a whore for statistics and constantly provided me with numbers for things like: eighty-five percent of all small businesses go broke in their first year of operations; most owner/operators of any business work an average of fifty hours a week all year long; the unemployment rate in B.C. is twenty-one percent; most men with a grade eleven education and no trade make under $35,000 dollars a year—blah, blah, blah. I couldn't argue with all of his statistics and this very convincing package wrapped in marijuana leaves. I'd eventually calm down and see the light.

Pot was a good thing; it was useful and innocuous and not our fault that a bunch of self-serving, conservative, booze-swilling, misinformed politicians made it illegal. After all, we used to hang people for being black. We used to forbid women to vote or drink in a pub. We used to burn witches. Just because a law is a law does not make it right or fair.

Booze, the most easily accessible and widely abused drug of the twentieth century, was illegal during Prohibition but managed to become completely legal, glorified and on top. The government profits so hugely from the tax on liquor that its harmful effects are ignored. Cigarette packages now come with standard warnings that you can look forward to death or disease from ingesting them, but the government continues to cash in on the unfortunate consumers that are hooked. Hopefully, some day soon, the world will realize how ludicrous our war on drugs is and politicians will come to their senses and legalize pot.

* * *

As September embraced us, warm and yellow and red, my plants were some of the nicest we owned. Most of the air surveillance in our area had stopped, but I was anxious to bring in my crop. Early in the month, I rented a house, hired Sherry to help me clip and harvested ten pounds.

My paranoia turned to welcome relief as news of an arrest traveled through our neighborhood. A woman my age, with a similar address, had been busted for growing pot. Although I had never met her, my heart raced and my arms broke out in goose bumps when

142

Michael relayed the story. I felt so terrible for her and yet incredibly lucky to have brought my plants in safely. I hated the police for arresting housewives for growing on their farms.

Most female growers that I knew cultivated pot because they smoked it. Often, their boyfriend or husband worked away, or was unemployed and unable to afford such luxuries; and by growing their own pot they were being independent. Surely, there were more important crimes being committed that required police attention.

I felt the scrape of the law. I'd always believed that somehow things were being exaggerated in the Pot World; they didn't really arrest ladies and take them to jail and fingerprint them and book them…for growing a little pot? That was just on those *COPS* shows in the US, where they're all conservative, religious and power-hungry. I was angry. More time and money was being wasted on the government's futile war on drugs—how dare they?

* * *

Michael did manage to harvest eighty-five pounds that fall. Not bad, considering the misfortune of many other growers. Jacob came in at three pounds, half of which he owed Michael. Mathew had eight pounds, five less than his previous year. Billy-Bob came in at two and a half pounds but did well collecting his rental fees from other growers. And some growers had two-hundred-pound years—guys on dripper systems.

Michael's latest obsession was a thirst for technical knowledge to improve outdoor growing. I knew the next experiment would involve new people and a lot of expensive equipment. I dreaded this and promised myself not to dwell on it until spring.

We spent most of the fall with me at the new house working with the crew and Michael harvesting and looking after Daisy. Our new house sucked up money like she always had but finally started to look inviting.

Rob Hudson started coming around to the new house and the rental place that we still lived in. We had both distanced ourselves from Rob and his wife, as they seemed to be sliding deeper down the rabbit hole. Her drinking had actually earned Liza the title of town drunk, and Rob was on and off crack cocaine, supporting his habit any way he could.

The saddest thing about Rob and Liza was that they had two young children who were suffering. They fought in front of them and got messed up on drugs and booze in front of them. They both lied and cheated their way through the miserable, blurry lives they had created for themselves. Rob was coming around because he needed money, and he figured Michael would be the guy to give it to him.

I was at the new house painting when Rob surprised me. I was just emerging from the hidden room as he appeared at the top of the hole. Desperate to get him away from our secret room, I ushered him outside and locked the door behind us.

"Is Michael around? I need to talk to him." Rob asked. "Hey, Liza's out in the truck with your Christmas present." Rob gestured towards a beat-up truck, a phony, strained smile crossing his sunken, ashen face.

I told him where to find Michael and snuck back into the house through another door. Rob and Liza didn't buy us Christmas presents; something was up. I ignored Rob and his skinny little wife, who was skulking around our house looking for a place to put our gift. Just as I started back to work, my dad called, as Michael sat outside with the desperate couple.

"They brought you guys a present, eh? I'd bet you anything they're probably out there buttering Michael up for a loan," Dad guessed, right on the money.

Let's just say Rob was angry when Michael told him that he couldn't and wouldn't lend him any money. Rob broke down and cried about how he had written $1700-worth of bad checks for Christmas presents and needed money in his account that day. This only infuriated Michael, and the answer was still no. Rob and Liza walked back towards their truck after he asked them to leave.

I guess Rob just didn't get it—he couldn't take no for an answer. Michael pulled into the driveway of the rental house to check his room, and there was Rob's truck. Rob stepped out slowly and approached, head and shoulders hunched. He devoured the insides of his mouth in silence as he waited for Michael's full attention. Again he turned on the tears; and Michael truly felt sorry for him, but not sorry enough to lend him money. The broken man with the crack cocaine habit the size of Texas and all those bad checks waiting to haunt him left empty-handed, four days before Christmas. Rob never spoke to us again.

Things were far enough along at our new house for Christmas to be set as the goal to move in. Against many odds, we moved in December 22nd. Daisy and I were thrilled, and Michael guardedly happy. He still hated the house that had caused us so much heartache and confusion. We put the hidden room into action, planting the biggest, greediest dope room I'd ever seen.

That first room was really special for many reasons, one of them being the sheer size of the plants. Michael had never grown such huge, beautiful dope indoors. The room was headed for greatness, and we couldn't wait to harvest our just rewards.

YEAR EIGHT, 1999

Busted and Desperate

On March 3rd, Michael headed outside to warm up the car to drive Daisy to her weekly ballet lesson. It was unusually cold and bitter for March. Wood smoke hung thickly in the air around the house, and dirty patches of snow clung to the frozen ground. Michael pulled the collar of his coat up around his neck and stepped out the front door.

A police car drove into the yard, followed closely by another and then a third. One of the eight cops who were suddenly present asked, "Are you Michael Hokenson?"

Michael calmly admitted who he was and was handed a search warrant. He read it slowly, trying to gather his wits and absorb what was happening. He asked politely, smirking, "Would you guys mind coming back tomorrow?"

One cop giggled at the question and was bombarded by dirty looks from most of the others. Michael asked if he could quickly take his daughter to her ballet lesson and come right back, but an officer informed him that if they found marijuana in the house he would be under arrest and not driving anywhere.

Doomed, Michael was escorted back into the house. He phoned my dad, who had just been visiting and was only a few miles down the road. He rushed back to take Daisy to her lesson and offered to take her to the farm for the night. Meanwhile, Michael was interrogated about where his marijuana room was as the police ripped our house apart.

It was obvious we had been turned in. The Love Shack was torn apart within minutes after the arrival of the eager Mounties. The barn and other outbuildings, which had no pot in them at all, were completely ignored. However, the hidden room gave the police a challenge.

Michael was repeatedly asked where the room was as he sat quietly on the couch while the search dragged on for almost an hour. He later told me he thought he had a small chance of them not finding the secret room, so he kept his mouth shut. Cops poured into the basement, ripping apart shelves and moving building materials; but they couldn't find the pot room. Eventually, and because the informant had told them about it, they located the trapdoor.

Michael's only question—"So, when's the last time you guys took down a fifty- or hundred-light Hells Angels room? Is busting little mom-and-pop shows really worth it?"—went glaringly unanswered.

Along with seven hundred clones in the Love Shack, all the mother plants and every piece of growing equipment, we lost our biggest, healthiest pot room to the police. We also lost all sorts of things from inside the house: our passports, a thank-you letter from my little sister, bills, income tax files, all our money, books and magazines about growing pot and, of course, pot. Dried pot, wet pot, Tony's pot (all bagged and ready for sale), pot seeds, my Ronnie stash—all gone. Michael was taken to jail, and it was my turn to be arrested.

Dad reached me on my cell phone as I drove home from an antique auction, loaded down with junk. I started laughing this uncontrollable, detached laugh and couldn't stop for a few minutes. Tony, sitting beside me clutching his purchase of the day, looked close to tears.

"This is bad. This is very bad," he announced quietly. "Oh, God, is Michael all right? Is he in jail? Why are you laughing? This is not funny, it's serious!"

Dad calmly informed me I was going to be arrested and had two choices about how to proceed: go home and be arrested or turn myself in at the police station on the way home. He also told me there were a lot of cops at our house going through my drawers and wearing their big, dirty cop boots in the house, He suggested I go home and have a firsthand look at what was going on.

I dropped a pale, flustered Tony off at home and headed to my house to face the music. I sat in my car for a minute, watching the surreal scene through the foggy windows. I could see the outlines of people moving throughout house—policemen looking for evidence. The memory of a helicopter hovering over the house that morning, loud and directly overhead, filtered through the confusion in my brain and settled in the pit of my stomach. I had off-handedly joked to Henrietta, "God, that helicopter sure is low. It sounds like it's right on top of our house. If I was a paranoid person, I'd think it was after us."

If I had acted on the fleeting feeling instead of joking about it and doing nothing, we could have emptied the house and avoided this bust. It was fate; I had let it happen.

After I pounded on the locked door to be let into my own house, I was promptly arrested. It was so unlike how I thought it would be. (Thankfully, I wasn't outside in my patch; or I'd have been nude.) Big, militant cops with brush-cut hair and tidy moustaches lectured me on the evils of marijuana. I accepted the challenge to debate but was outnumbered, yelled at and told it was "very bad" and it led to "other things." I refused to answer any of their pointless questions and sat down on the stairs awaiting further instructions.

My silence only lasted seconds. Frustrated and angry, I asked them why they didn't go out and arrest a real criminal and stop wasting taxpayers' dollars on these small-time plant busts. Surely, there was a rapist or a burglar or a murderer they could be tracking down. It seemed almost silly that I was now a criminal. I saw myself as a housewife who volunteered at kindergarten and just happened to love gardening.

I was followed around my house as I insisted on grabbing some things in preparation for my night in jail. One nasty old cop with snow-white hair was in my bedroom, going through all of my underwear drawers—I guess looking for pot. Two undercover drug-squad cops that looked like a couple of losers on a night out at the local pub were eating Kentucky Fried Chicken in the kitchen. They wore tight, faded blue jeans and had long, scraggly hair, and one had an earring. They were polite and gentle and wanted information, but I was fresh out of manners. I refused to be helpful, much less civil, and told them what I thought of our drug laws.

It was time to go. The uniformed Silver Fox drove me to the police station in a car fueled by testosterone. As I sat in the back, a thought occurred to me. Being a cop was a job, and cops should execute their daily tasks just as any other workingman or woman. A doctor or nurse working in an emergency room doesn't throw her arms in the air and scream when a patient comes in with a severed limb. A schoolteacher doesn't run to a corner and cry when a student is rude or defiant. Why, then, are police officers always so worked up and bursting with adrenaline when they make a simple arrest? Shouldn't it be a routine part of the job carried out calmly and professionally? Why was this white-haired bastard taunting me and lecturing me and driving in a manner that was dangerous and unacceptable?

That was about it for my arrest. Once I was safely inside my concrete-walled cell, no one bothered me. I guess because I was a snotty, argumentative bitch instead of a whimpering, blubbering, terrified member of the weaker sex, I was never so much as talked to. I got no food, a phone call that informed me my lawyer was at the hockey game, no interview and no conversation once inside my cell. I just did sit-ups and read magazines until they let me out.

With an ignorant remark about my future rolling off his tongue, the Silver Fox handed me a little envelope containing the dangerous possessions he had removed from me before putting me in the cell: two pieces of Kleenex, my wedding ring and a necklace. Had I been more creative, I could have smuggled in the Kleenex, shoved it up my nostrils and died of suffocation. The wedding ring clearly could have been used to stab the nice matron who brought me magazines; and the necklace, I suppose, could have been used to hang someone providing they didn't weigh over two pounds.

Absurd would be the one word I would use to best describe my arrest and night in jail. And I still didn't consider myself a criminal or have any intention of changing the way I led my life. I felt anger at myself for being apathetic and not writing politicians about our ridiculous laws against marijuana and other drugs.

Michael had been busy while I'd suffered through hours of dated *MacLean's* and *Reader's Digest* magazines. The police had interviewed him, and the undercover boss asked him to become an informant in exchange for the charges against us being dropped. Michael found this request disgusting and sleazy, assuming that was probably how we had ended up in jail in the first place. He insisted that the only people he knew growing pot were doing so in the closet of a house trailer and probably not worth their effort. He refused to inform them of anything and asked that he be charged and released.

Both Michael and I were charged with production of a controlled substance and possession for the purpose of trafficking.

My poor, tired father waited outside the jail for hours and calmly drove us home in a raging snowstorm. Tony came over immediately, and the three of us went over the events of the last ten hours. I told Michael about the helicopter, but he didn't care. The question was, *why* did we get busted? Who turned us in? Why would anyone turn us in? What about the other house—did they know about it, too? Why were there undercover drug cops from another city present at our arrest? How much did they really know? Were we being watched? Was our house under surveillance? On and on the unanswered questions plagued us.

Michael remembered that the power bills for both houses had been on the counter with a wad of money when the police arrived. He had intended to pay them while Daisy was at dance class. As he sat in his jail cell he promised himself that if when he returned home the power bill for the rental house was gone he would immediately go and take the grow room down.

Even though it was one o'clock in the morning, we drove to the rental house and ripped out hundreds of immature marijuana plants. Dirt flew all around us as we struggled to empty the tables of the trouble-causing little plants at top speed. Tony drove to the river and dumped everything while Michael and I gathered some of the equipment and other incriminating objects.

When we returned home, I grabbed my vacuum cleaner and went into a cleaning frenzy, sweating, grunting and panting. Like a woman who's just been raped, I felt a burning need to cleanse my house of police dirt and energy. The floors were muddy and scuffed from the eight pairs of booted feet tracking across them for five hours. Every cupboard, drawer and container in the house had been opened; and everything seemed slightly out of place. I tired around four in the morning, satisfied that my house was clean and germ-free.

Michael and I lay awake for what was left of the stormy night, whispering and wondering. We imagined all sorts of horrible things: the house was bugged, the phone was tapped, someone was watching us from across the road, someone out there hated us and had turned us in, some new person we'd met was an undercover cop and God knows what else. We planned to pick Daisy up early enough from my parents to get her back home and at her bus stop so that nothing seemed different to her. We had to get some sleep.

With Daisy at school, we headed back to the rental house and dismantled everything with the help of some sympathetic friends. By dinnertime that night Michael had given notice on the house, disconnected the power and moved everything to a safe place. The next order of business was to hire a lawyer and put in another grow room to pay his bill.

Just like riding a horse, a dedicated pot grower has no choice but to hop back into the saddle and ride out the storm. A friend of Jacob's, a huge bodybuilder named Kevin who was becoming an accomplished grower, came to our rescue with enough clones to start a new room. Surprisingly, the police had left us two lights, a tracker, some timers and fans and the bottoms of several large mother plants. We, of course, interpreted this as an okay to start growing again. Four nights after our being released from jail, the hidden room was full of marijuana.

About two weeks after our arrest, a neighbor we'd recently met dropped by late one night to tell us that two cops had been seen sneaking around our rental house. They had either finally looked at the power bills and noticed there were two or the informant told them we had another grow house somewhere.

The plainclothes off-duty cops peered in the windows with flashlights and circled the house, pulling on anything loose. This was a questionable way for them to obtain evidence, though it didn't matter, anyway. All they saw was a spotless, empty house. There were no exhaust fans blowing pot-smelling air, no blacked-out windows to hide slivers of light; and best of all, there was no marijuana growing. We thanked the neighbor for the information and went back to bed.

The only lawyer we knew specialized in real estate. The one recommended to us was an old acquaintance of Michael's named Tommy Dodge. From the moment I met Mr. Dodge he reminded me of a Hobbit. Short and pudgy with thick, messy hair, he shuffled around in crumpled clothes with little chunks of food in them but had a brilliant mind hidden beneath this deceiving exterior. Even his car was tiny and Hobbit-like. He had bought the first house Michael ever owned and turned it into a law office.

Tommy had quite a reputation. A brilliant criminal lawyer specializing in drug defenses, his career had been blemished by personal tragedy. Mr. Dodge lived an alternative lifestyle that included nude solstice parties on his private island and experimenting with mind-altering drugs. Partway through his career, he lost his wife to cancer and was understandably depressed and devastated. He battled with alcoholism and often fell off the wagon after years of sobriety. Yet, amidst the highs and lows of life and work, Tommy's lawyer-mind was sharp. He took our case.

It was comforting to talk to a good lawyer. We learned so much in our first meeting with Tommy that, in one sense, it had been beneficial to get busted. We finally knew how it all worked. People all around us were always telling stories of phone taps and surveillance and living these silly, paranoid delusions. Michael and I tried not to believe stuff like this, but who could honestly know?

Just as Tim had imagined the guys at Fag Hiker were cops, people imagined that their small-time grow operations were under police investigation. In reality, the police were swamped with drug tips and had nowhere near the budget or manpower to investigate every little thing. It was estimated that one in five houses in our community was a grow house; the number is similar for the entire province. In our case, a fink had simply turned us in.

Tommy promised that, when he got the police report, he would do his best to help us figure out who it was. That was the worst thing about being turned in—who had done this, and would they do it again?

In the weeks that followed, Michael and I eliminated a lot of people from our lives. We had a strong feeling that Rob had probably turned us in for money, revenge or to save himself from an embarrassing arrest for cocaine possession or drunk driving. But we couldn't be sure who the rat was, so we put the word out that Michael had quit growing.

We stayed at home licking our wounds for months. We had never been much for going out or socializing, but we did have to buy groceries and frequent the hardware store. Michael refused to leave the house—I went out for everything we needed and felt no shame or guilt.

Daisy's bus driver never treated us the same in the aftermath of our bust. He was cold, rude and silent, a shock to both Michael and I. Our one and only close neighbor referred to us as "drug dealers" from then on. He had always liked us both and had told me how much he admired how hard I worked in the yard and how happy he was with the improvements we'd made to the rundown little farm. His wife spent her days shut in the house drinking a bottle of vodka almost every day, but he couldn't bring himself to have any respect for the dope-dealing criminals he shared a fence line with.

Our house was very close to the road, and the whole neighborhood saw the numerous police cars, the B.C. Hydro truck and boxes of equipment and plants being packed up and driven out of the yard. Gossip flew. The paper reported a totally fictitious and exaggerated amount of pot with an estimated street value of two hundred thousand dollars and growing equipment worth one hundred thousand. If this had been true we'd have sold everything and taken a year off.

But since ours was a pot-growing community, most people were either sympathetic or nonchalant about our infamous careers. As a study in human behavior, this was a wonderful opportunity to find out about people's true colors.

153

* * *

APRIL 17—We made another appearance in court today. The system is frustrating, each wasted day costing $2,500. We showed up, ready to proceed, only to be sent home near the end of the day when it became apparent that the day was over-booked— again. The day began at 9:30 and by lunch there had been two recesses. Nothing ever seems to get done with postponement after postponement until it's time for another break. Then, the day is over. All the while, Michael and I sit on the hard, uncomfortable chairs, observing.

I have to admit we were both entertained by the courtroom dramas and the people-watching. Most of the alleged criminals were male, unbathed, unemployed, uneducated and usually with a few teeth missing. Most of the alleged offences committed involved our favorite national drug, alcohol.

Police officers were spat at, urinated on, verbally insulted or physically assaulted by the toothless perpetrators. Some of the men had stolen cars, vandalized private or public property, beaten up family members or brawled in a public place. A few women had shoplifted, committed petty crimes or been arrested for driving under the influence.

And there we sat, clean, polite, semi-educated, mainly law-abiding citizens, waiting our turn at justice. We prayed that when we finally got our day in court the wise and intelligent judge would see us for the pillars of society we really were.

Our court date was postponed for another seven months.

* * *

Michael planned his outdoor year as usual. It was as if he had a huge magic bag from which he pulled an endless supply of helpers. Part of the magic was that the bag only supplied helpers with drug and alcohol addictions. Even when he thought he had found the perfect employee, a helper who had licked his problem with booze or faced his drug-induced demons, the magic bag only contained damaged goods.

The problem was that he couldn't stop looking in the bag—it was too easy, and it was bottomless. But when you're in the Pot World, your choice of part-time laborers is limited, and good help really is hard to find.

Damon Murdock was scratching and kicking his way out of a deep, fetid hole. He was thirty-five but looked remarkably younger, a massive mop of black, curly hair partly hiding his pale, freckled face. Michael found him just as he was surfacing, living in his mother's basement with the help of a steady welfare check.

Damon had worked for a big-shot pot grower for the past two years, his job ending when a small-time bike gang had been sold maps to the bigshot's areas. Damon was camping in one of the large patches when everything went wrong. The boss was held at gunpoint and forced to cut down his own pot and help the thieves pack it out of the bush. Someone got word to Damon, who fled on foot and was never paid or compensated for an entire year of hard work.

But such is life in the drug business. His boss was actually shot and hospitalized and ended up with nothing himself. Full of anger and self-pity, Damon immediately turned to drugs but somehow found the strength to quit as quickly as he had started.

Michael had known both Damon and his employer for more than fifteen years. Everyone in our small community had heard the story of the bikers holding a pot grower and his wife hostage and the subsequent shooting in the bush.

Damon was hired and put up in a house at our expense. Tony and I drove to Damon's mother's to gather the new employee. He bounded out of the modest little house in a T-shirt that read "How Think Do You Stoned I Am?" and pointy-toed black cowboy boots that never should have been popular. I groaned at the sight of him but reminded myself not to be too judgmental. We packed his belongings into the truck and headed for home.

What he lacked in style and education, Damon seemed to make

up for with hard work. He was incredibly strong and willing, and I really had no complaints about this particular helper. He had no vehicle; so when we needed him to work, we drove to his house and picked him up. His new home was tidy and decorated whimsically with burlap coffee sacks and science fiction memorabilia. Michael had set up a grow room in the basement and they planned to split the proceeds fifty-fifty. Damon transplanted clones and helped with spring start-up, his life taking shape for the first time in months.

On May 25th, Jacob's younger brother John was planning to propose to his girlfriend. Twenty people were invited to the surprise engagement party, and Michael had booked the night off for himself and Damon. On our way to the party, we gave Damon a ride to town and dropped him at a mall. We told him to call us on our cell phone around midnight so we could all drive home together. We never got the call.

May 26th had been scheduled for planting Michael's acreage. We checked Damon's house on the way to the property, and there was no sign of him. Tony had been at John's party with us and had a bad feeling about Damon's not calling; he volunteered to help us plant the property. For the next four days we planted clones.

It was amazingly hot. We worked long hours prepping the holes and planted when the sun's rays relented and disappeared behind the violet mountains. We returned home exhausted and filthy every night and slept a few gratifying hours. Still no word from Damon.

We started to worry and finally called the hospital and Damon's mother. He was hiding in a flophouse less than a mile from where we had dropped him off six days earlier. His mother knew this only because he had tried to borrow money from her the day before we called.

Michael went to check the indoor room Damon had in his basement; it was dead. Not only was the room dead; but Damon had cut a hole in the wall, and the plants had gone back into a vegetative cycle before dying from lack of water. Most of Michael's help was usually fired after one season, but Damon broke the record previously held by Boomer for shortest tour of duty.

Eleven days after being dropped off, Damon returned. He begged for forgiveness, but Michael had everything under control and only spoke to him about entering a drug rehab program. He gave Damon three hundred clones, which he sold for three thousand dollars, and we didn't hear from him until late that fall.

I took a job with Jacob and Kevin to have cash coming in all spring. Oddly enough, Jacob had won me over, and I had come to love him like the little brother I never had.

Kevin was interesting. Years of gargantuan steroid use had caused him to become delusional; I found him fascinating. He had been in jail for a few years as a youth and bounced between relatives, having no father and a mother unfit to care for him. Short, insecure and angry, he had turned to bodybuilding.

By the time he was finished high school, Kevin's five-foot, five-inch frame packed a whopping two hundred pounds. His tiny dark head perched on his steroid-built neck, and arms as big as thighs protruded from his beefy shoulders. When Kevin walked, everything rubbed together. Piercing pale-blue eyes and a shrill, girl-like giggle topped off the very unique package.

* * *

> JUNE 2—*Never in my life have I enjoyed a job so thoroughly! My bosses are kind, easygoing, generous and fucking hilarious. They also respect my ability to grow pot. Most outdoor laborer jobs go to men. The pace is demanding and everything involves strength. Kevin and Jacob treated me like a princess my first day, but when I demanded equal pay for equal labor, they let me have it.*

The juice monkeys, as they lovingly referred to themselves, planned a monster-sized year. They bought plants called *monsters* and aimed for three thousand clones. Lost World, the newest area from last year, was slated to be the home of the massive grow.

When Billy had first discovered the mountaintop swamp, he said it felt like no one had ever been there—a secret, forgotten land. By the end of his first season there, Michael felt differently about Lost World. Other growers used the same access roads; and late in the year, a patch of plants in five-gallon buckets had appeared near the entrance to the swamp. This hadn't bothered Jacob at all, but Michael said he would never grow there again. Kevin had only grown indoors and thought the immense marshland was big enough for everyone.

The site preparation for Lost World was lengthy and difficult…

* * *

"Hey, Jacob, did you bring the sandwiches, man?"

"No. Shit, man, I thought you were making lunch."

Every day began the same. I was paid a daily rate of two hundred dollars, no matter what the day entailed. I would stand in Jacob's kitchen, our meeting place, lunch packed and ready to go, and watch the two massive young men carefully make ten or twelve sandwiches. Then, eight or nine juices and pops were added to the lunch along with yogurt, bananas, power bars, chewing tobacco, bottled water and numerous pastries. All this was packed into Kevin's ultra-expensive backpack before we headed out to the truck.

The ride into Lost World required a quad, so Jacob bought one. He also had a brand-new white Dodge pickup that never seemed to have the quad in it. So, the next order of business was loading the quad without the aid of a ramp. One person backed in close to a thorny, overgrown bank while the other took a run at the back of the truck. Eventually, the bike was loaded. Next, we dumped in work boots, bear mace, rain gear, shovels and picks, fertilizers and other growing supplies. After a quick snack, my bosses and I would be on the road.

The drive took just over half an hour, and Jacob and Kevin usually bantered back and forth or forced me to listen to their latest favorite songs. Jacob pretended he was the host of a syndicated talk show called *Mr. Wilderness*. He was the star of the show and knew everything there was to know about hunting, fishing, wildlife, birds and wilderness survival. Nothing could have been farther from the truth, and that was what made it so funny.

"Today, we're going to travel deep into the forest and learn about the mating habits of the red-breasted tree frog. Oh, I see there's a dip in the road. It's a good thing Mr. Wilderness is an excellent driver and…oh, shit! Fuck, Kevin, man, can you drive this hunk of shit and get us the hell out of the creek."

Jacob would smile his mega-watt smile as if the camera was in the cab and jump to safety while Kevin took the wheel. With a grinding of gears and general smashing and spinning that lease customers are famous for, Kevin would drive the truck out of the ditch. We'd continue up the de-activated road for several more miles and make the last part of the journey squashed together on the quad.

Once to the edge of the patch, we'd load our gear onto each other's backs and begin the long walk in. Lost World was wet, like all of Billy's areas. It was a giant bowl surrounded by jagged, snow-covered outcroppings of rock and the remains of massive, burned-out trees. The stumps were huge and either bleached like driftwood or as black as charcoal. Blueberry bushes filled the banks surrounding the alpine oasis.

We started digging holes near the middle of the swamp and branched out in several arms, following Jacob's lead. The morning was a time of productivity for the steroid-driven growers. All fueled up, both men would frantically dig until they needed food so badly they would have given up tanning and shaving for the promise of a tuna-and-sweet pickle sandwich. The packsack would be located and emptied, the two breathing a collective sigh of relief.

This would usually be about an hour into our arrival at the patch. Then, it was time for a head-dunk in the thick, smelly water to bring their body temperatures to a level close to normal.

Not exactly an expert on steroids, I have come to understand the drugs a bit. Steroids cause a slight increase in body temperature, appetite increase, diminished sex drive and mood swings that can make the user violent and short-fused. All that extra testosterone, in drugs that are intended for veterinarian use, do nothing positive for human beings—unless that neckless, unnatural physique can be considered good. I also understood that if I didn't keep working, not much would get done. Kevin and Jacob had power but virtually no endurance. Cardiovascular activity burns fat; and when you're all pumped up, you don't want to lose any of your hard-earned bulk.

Jacob's first fifty holes were all dug around the biggest blueberry bush I had ever seen.

"Hey, Mr. Wilderness, do you know that a bear is going to come and sit right on top of all of your plants while he eats blueberries off this huge bush?" I asked, snickering. I suggested filling the holes in to Jacob, and he sadly agreed after asking me if I was positive the shrub was a blueberry bush.

Meanwhile, Kevin was marking spots for holes ahead of us, scraping off the top layer of grass and earth to make it easier for Jacob to dig. After the first few hundred holes were dug, both novice growers admitted they were relieved that half of their clones had died.

The holes became much smaller as the days progressed. Reaching the lofty goal of fifteen hundred was going to be impossible. Both Kevin and Jacob had lost weight and yearned for a manicure, a body-wax, hairstreaks and a night out—anything other than the monotonous trips into the hot, fly-drenched swamp. I loved the money and the exercise that my summer job provided and was crushed if they called me to cancel a day's work.

By late July, Lost World was ready according to my employers. To get fifteen hundred tall, spindly clones deep into the swamp required some imaginative planning. Jacob built a stretcher out of plywood and two-by-fours with tall sides and four carrying handles. At the entrance to the swamp, the stretcher was loaded with six trays containing sixty or seventy sopping-wet clones each. I carried in the fifty-pound lunch and anything else we'd need for the day while Jacob and Kevin wrestled with the stretcher.

Jacob referred to the cumbersome vessel he had designed as a "crack whore," which always made us all giggle and have to stop moving. The guy at the front had to constantly yell directions to the guy at the back, who couldn't see anything but marijuana clones and the top rim of the crack whore. Each trip took about an hour one way, with numerous stops and a few position exchanges. Once in the patch, I'd stay alone and plant while another load of clones was transported.

The bucket patch from the previous year returned midway through the packing in of clones. Most of the buckets were directly in our path, making it difficult for us to get in with a full load. Each day, one of us would carefully move the plants aside and put them back in place before we left. Kevin left a note and a tray of clones for the unknown grower when some of his plants got sick during our first few days in the swamp. I was always so touched by this gesture and felt like there was hope for the world when I spent time with guys like Kevin and Jacob.

It took many long days to get the plants into their holes and watered in. The weather was relentlessly hot, which meant we had to wait until it cooled down before planting to prevent shock to the clones. Always in a hurry, the last thing my bosses wanted to do at the end of the day was work; and many plants died as quickly as we put them in, the roots not developed enough to withstand the slightest trauma.

The days blurred together, with everyone sore and sunburned; and there always seemed to be a bunch of unplanted trays at the end of the day. A new day would begin with replanting and trying to catch up from the day before—amazingly, both Kevin and Jacob laughed and joked their way through it all.

Near the end of planting, we dug huge, muddy trenches near the pooling water, scooping dirt and muck high up out of the swamp. Both exhausted growers wanted the tedious job finalized. Every remaining clone was shoved into the muck, only inches from the next.

"Voila! Finished at last!" Kevin beamed and asked, "So, what do you think?"

I wanted to say something, but there was no point. If they couldn't see that a plant supposed to reach a height of eight feet, with a pound of pot on it, would need a bit more room, then what else couldn't they see? I felt their whole year was in big trouble, starting with planting an unproven strain of very unhealthy clones. The holes were small and uninviting, either full of mud and roots and rock or directly in the swamp, drowning. With good weather and a little luck, though, you never know. I smiled at my bosses and started packing up.

* * *

Michael and Mathew were tired of paying Billy-Bob's hefty fee every fall, so they decided to go separate ways and try out some new areas on their own. Mathew had ballooned to over three hundred pounds, and Michael's worst fear was that he would have a heart attack in the bush and there would be no way of getting him out.

Michael was counting on his property and hoped to build a dripper system over the course of the season. If he could cut his maintenance time down, that would leave him more time to spend with his family; and he could plant more wild grow areas. The only question remaining was, who would be the fall guard?

Damon had been perfect for the job after having spent several seasons in bush camps. With this option dissipated, Michael dreaded having to be his own guard at a time of year when he was harvesting, hiring clippers, making deals and just generally being consumed by the stress of his illegal profession.

In June a friend of ours from Vancouver came to visit for the weekend, and he brought along a couple of his friends. Like pennies from heaven, Michael's prayers for a capable guard were answered and fell into his lap.

There is no sugar coating who these friends were—they were triad gang members. Of course, no one initially mentioned to me that these new and interesting ethnically diverse guys were gangsters. At least, no one mentioned it to me until it was too late. I thought, wow, these guys sure have a lot of brothers, not yet understanding gang lingo and their whole way of life. I liked Viet and Azim and found all of their stories fascinating.

Azim had come to Canada on a phony passport while attempting to travel to Holland. A young soldier from Afghanistan, he had fled his country after serving seven years in the army. He fought the rebels for his government and eventually found himself taking orders from a Russian who had been put in charge of his squadron. With shoes that didn't fit and an ulcer gnawing away at his stomach, he was denied a

162

cigarette one day, the only thing he'd asked for in a long time. At that moment, Azim decided he could no longer serve his harsh new supervisor and a country that treated its people so poorly.

He hated the Russians, and his war-torn country was in ruins all around him. He fled on foot through the mountains and sold his rifle for the price of a passport. The man who gave him a new identity taught him how to say "freedom." He told Azim if anything started to go wrong, use the word. Over and over he practiced: freedom, freedom, freedom.

Somehow, Azim landed in Vancouver, B.C. Customs and immigration detained him for days, having difficulty believing his story. All he would do was nod his head and say, "Freedom. Freedom, freedom." He was eventually released onto the street during an uncommon west coast blizzard—cold, hungry and penniless.

Azim walked. Despite his having no grasp of English and nowhere to go, it started to sink in that he was in Canada, and he was free. Massive snowflakes gave way to freezing rain and soaked through his clothes as he continued. His skin was completely numb and his whole body shook involuntarily by the time he reached a tall, imposing structure covered in ivy. A church.

Azim entered the warm building full of lighted candles and intricate stained glass. He did not want to ask for anything so he waited quietly, praying that someone would offer him a meal. During the day he prayed, and at night he left the sanctuary of the church and wandered the streets of downtown Vancouver. After three days with no food, he finally ate a hamburger because someone offered it to him.

The first of many menial jobs Azim took was on the loading docks. For weeks he worked as part of a crew who all shared English as a first or second language. At some point in the day, guys would inevitably stare and point at him, breaking into howls of laughter. Azim laughed, too, not knowing what else to do and desperately trying to fit in. Eventually, he picked up a bit of English, and his friends at work explained that he was wearing girls' jeans—the tight eighties ones with zippers up the ankles.

When Azim tells this story in his thickly accented, animated voice, it always ends up reducing everyone to hysterics. Picturing a tough, seasoned soldier with a bushy black moustache and muscular physique scurrying around the loading docks surrounded by burly men named Savo and Butch in his tight girls' jeans is just plain funny. And Azim had a hundred stories like that one; he saw humor in everything and understood how people could laugh at him.

Viet was a child refugee from North Vietnam who crowded onto a homemade boat with twelve others seeking a new world. Eventually, he and part of his family ended up in Toronto. Unable to speak English and too young to work, he entered a gang by the age of twelve and moved up the chain of command. When we met Viet, he had just served six years in prison for murder, a sentence he served for his gang.

At twenty-two, the only thing Viet knew was crime. He developed a phobia of being alone after his release from prison and was always with a brother or two and rigorously attached to his cell phone. Tough, good-looking and aggressive, Viet was the perfect gangster.

The last real job Azim had was driving taxi. He made about eighty dollars for a twelve-hour shift. It wasn't so much the money, he told us, as the abuse that led him to quit. Called everything from a "dirty Paki" to a "fucking rag-head" despite not even being from the country these insults were intended for, the final straw was being told to carry some huge, fat woman in a wheelchair.

He couldn't lift the behemoth out of the chair, her corpulent ass squashed into the vinyl and stuck as if with cement. After he had tried his best, the woman's companion screamed a tirade of insults as Azim let go of her and the wheelchair in defeat.

"I no have to put with this shit!" he declared and walked off the job and into the age of wonder. He met Viet and joined one of the largest gangs in the world.

Viet and Azim ran a speed lab together. In a rented house in a suburb of Vancouver, they oversaw the production of methamphetamine while dabbling in other illustrious ventures. In early 1999 the house was raided by police and shut down after only three months of operation.

Azim's ulcer was eating away at him; and he admitted he needed a change of pace, a holiday, a visit to the country. And that's when our friend brought him to our house. He knew there was always the chance good old Michael was hiring help for spring start-up or guarding.

Boomer had proven to be disastrous, as had Willy and Vern and anyone else who'd attempted the job. Michael had threatened to move to his property for the entire two months of budding season if he couldn't find someone serious this year. After much discussion and careful planning, Azim agreed to guard and work for the months of August and September. Viet would remain in Vancouver and oversee their group ventures. Michael could maintain all of his other areas while the gang looked after his property. Azim would be paid ten thousand dollars per month and given days off whenever he needed.

On August 1st, Azim arrived with one brother, a twenty-three-year-old named Rinshu, and a German shepherd. Michael's bus had been replaced with a new travel trailer, and the boys set to fixing up the place. They pruned trees, mowed the grass, built a few fire pits and stocked up on necessities. Every day, the plants were watered, tied down, sprayed or pruned. Azim was doing an incredible job. And at night when their work was done, the brothers would have target practice with the arsenal of weapons they had brought along.

I don't like guns, and I don't know much about them. I've never seen so many guns and bullets as I did in the trailer that year—handguns, shotguns, sawed-off shotguns, automatic rifles and cases of ammunition. The trailer looked like a scene from *The Matrix*. I prayed that no one tried to steal pot that fall.

Michael figured that the obvious presence of armed guards at his property would deter thievery of any form. Still, just having a car drive in and out and fires burning and lights on were what he was really after. Azim had sworn that no one would be harmed with a gun; this was paramount with Michael. If a thief was caught, he could be beat up or scared with a gun that wasn't loaded. Roger, the giant German shepherd was mean-looking enough to scare away most people. Serious thieves would be dealt with accordingly.

"Hey, sis, you want to shoot guns?" Azim asked excitedly the first time I came to visit him on the job.

"I don't think so, Azim. I've never shot a gun before. I don't like guns—they make me nervous." Not as nervous, though, as being pressured to do something by a heavily armed triad gangster. I had a lesson with a handgun and failed miserably. The empty pop bottle I aimed for sat motionless in a tree as I fired all around it. Happy I had at least tried, Azim let the pressure off. Tony had come with me that day and thought the whole scene was quite amusing.

"Hey, bro, do you want to do some really crazy drug with us?" Azim asked the virgin Tony. "It's from Wancouwer, man, really crazy. Make you go cuckoo."

Tony thought about the offer for a second, a broad grin breaking out on his face, "Sure. I'll do some E with you guys." This would be Tony's third drug trip in twenty-three years. He had tried drinking once and threw up on Carmella at a Canada Day dance. Pot made him silent and sleepy, but ecstasy made him godlike. I was just happy he was fitting in.

"Good, bro, that's good, man, because Rinshu, here—man, he doesn't do no crazy shit like that. He just does the weed. I don't want to do shit alone because I might get all cuckoo." Azim put his index finger to his temple as he mentioned this, but Tony was willing to babysit a crazy gangster high on ecstasy.

Tony's soft-spoken, shy nature was respected by all the brothers, who had only one complaint about him—he was twenty-three and still a virgin. They found this downright offensive and constantly offered to buy him any girl he wanted. He settled for a hit of really crazy E and the company of two highly entertaining men with stories from all around the world. I told Tony I'd be back for him the next day and drove home to make dinner.

Kevin and Jacob visited the greenhorn farmers/guards whenever they had time and played cards or told stories and sampled the wonderful cooking that both men were capable of. Carmella, who lived only a few miles up the road, often brought over special coffee or desserts in exchange for drugs and entertainment. The whole neighborhood knew Michael had some serious guards living on his property. Not one stranger ventured down the long grassy driveway all summer. Other than the sounds of gunfire and Roger's occasional barking, the dope-laden property was quiet.

I worked about once a week doing maintenance for the girls, as I'd come to call Kevin and Jacob. Their plants needed extra fertilizer and staking because they were weak and spindly. Every time I saw the plants they looked worse. I knew something was wrong but couldn't bring myself to tell the ladies—and what good would it have done, anyway?

Kevin was convinced they were going to be millionaires. He planned on buying a Hummer and owning his own airplane. Jacob, having grown outdoors before unsuccessfully, was not quite as delusional as his partner. He also took a fraction of the steroids Kevin did, making him a more sane person overall.

That summer was hot; the forest was alive with bears, deer and pot growers. Michael was on edge constantly, worrying about whether or not he would pull through for his family. I felt myself drifting away from the love of my life for the first time since we had seen each other in the field at the music festival. It seemed like a hundred years ago when both of us had been free and optimistic. Now, we had this farm and a child and mortgages and bills and cats and llamas and the looming court date in October.

I just couldn't make myself upset or worried. I thought that whatever was going to happen to us was beyond our control. I didn't mind being powerless. I thought we would get what we deserved in life, and if we had to start again it wouldn't be the end of the world. Maybe the end of the Pot World was something I could live with. So, I chose not to talk about it or worry about it, while Michael drank our troubles like a poisoned wine. Everyone noticed the change.

* * *

AUGUST 7—*I miss the constant jokes and spoofs. My new husband is serious and negative. We've both thrown ourselves into work, falling into bed at night too tired and sore to make conversation. I spend all*

*of my days off in my garden or with Daisy and go
out as often as I can, staying out late, dancing,
laughing and indulging in the pleasures of drugs
and alcohol. Michael is not ready. He stays very
close to home when not tending to his gardens and
only enjoys time spent with Daisy or alone.*

*I wonder if we'll be together forever. I wonder if
any married couple is truly happy. I feel like
throwing something at Michael or hitting him...but
mostly I don't feel like being around him anymore.
Obviously, I wasn't cut out for marriage but who the
hell is? But then I think of Daisy. She has a
wonderful dad and I owe it to her to try a bit
harder. I'll ride it out and see what happens.*

Ronnie Love died at his kitchen table of heart failure, fluid around his
lungs and cirrhosis of the liver. It was August 15th; he was forty-three
years old. Michael was shocked, depressed and, in a way, angry with
Ronnie. I was angry with Ronnie, too, for slowly killing himself with
booze in front of his friends and family. Ronnie's parents asked
Michael to give the eulogy for his boyhood friend, and composing the
passionate speech consumed his days leading up to the funeral.

The nights grew colder, and the beaches surrounding our home
became quiet and deserted. Fall always made Michael melancholy. He
had grown up summering at his family's lakeside cabin, and there he
had experienced the most important events of his youth: his first
girlfriend, learning to water ski, the tattoo his father nearly killed him
for and countless sunny days lazing on the beach with his friends.

But always at the end of summer came the sadness, the emptiness.
Only he and Ronnie were left to sit alone on the sand and stare into
the clear autumn sky. The endless dark water was still and calm,
devoid of boats and swimmers.

This fall of 1999, the melancholy feeling never came. A depressed
Michael dreaded October and all that might come with it. He barely
noticed the change in the sky that always made him ache with
sadness. We read the police report again, having filed it away for

months, to familiarize ourselves with our case.

The police suggested to the Crown that we be fined twenty thousand dollars, a virtually unheard-of amount for the crime of running two small grow rooms. The police suggested Michael should really be punished for raising a daughter in "this kind of environment." The report also stated that we lived in a Quonset-style hut with heated coils in the floor (this we never figured out), that a police officer was in our yard four years earlier and saw what he thought may have been marijuana growing and a lot of other weird things, most of which were untrue and had us flabbergasted. We actually thought they made a mistake—they must have been referring to some other people and mixed up our name with theirs.

This, our lawyer Tommy told us, was good. There was really nothing valid or incriminating in the entire report besides the statement by the unknown informant. By refusing to give the identity of the informant, the police had very little evidence for obtaining a search warrant.

We brought in our harvest and readied for court simultaneously. Azim was preparing to go back to the city and wanted to take us out for an extravagant farewell dinner. With two days left to go, ten of us went to the best restaurant our community had to offer. We dined gangster-style, ordering huge trays of tequila shots in the classy fine-dining atmosphere. I don't think the white-toweled waiter had ever had the pleasure of delivering such a plethora of liquor in the elegant dining room that catered to German and Asian bus tours filled with seniors.

After dinner, we decided to hit the local pub, something we rarely did. In the parking lot of the dingy, rundown watering hole, Azim fumbled in the trunk for just the right weapon.

"Azim, what are you doing there, buddy?" Jacob calmly inquired, patting his foreign brother on the back.

"Just getting my piece, bro." Azim informed us as he looked over several different weapons.

"Piece of what, man? A gun? Here? No, you don't need that in here. You're in the country, no one here is like that." A convincing Jacob walked into the little pub with his arm linked in Azim's. "Relax, buddy. It's all about love, man; it's all good."

An hour later, we spilled out of the pub into the cool September night. Michael had gone home earlier, and only Tony and I remained with the brothers as Kevin and Jacob drove away. We had one vehicle among the four of us, and Tony and I needed to go in the opposite direction from Rinshu and Azim.

Tony, always sober, got us back to his car at the restaurant where the evening had begun. We drove home slowly, my hangover already setting in with a pounding headache and dry mouth. Oh, how I hated booze and myself for trying to drink so much of it. I passed out in the sanctum of Tony's backseat and awoke to Michael carrying me up the stairs to our bed.

Azim insisted to a semi-sober Rinshu that he would drive back home to the trailer and there was no arguing with him. Four miles from the driveway, he drove off the road. The car plunged down a twenty-foot bank and came to rest against a tree. The car belonged to a brother, and both men felt horrible about crashing it. Uninjured, they walked home, with Azim staggering and full of stupid laughter.

By the time they reached the gate, the laughter had been replaced with guilt and shame. The ulcers gnawed and ached in the pit of Azim's stomach, a welcome feeling for a man who felt he deserved pain for his shameful act. The brothers stayed up all night cleaning and packing their things. In the early morning, they got the mangled car towed and headed back to the city. We got a phone call that night telling us they were home safe. Apologetic and humble, Azim was brief. We wouldn't see any of our new friends until weeks later when Azim returned to get paid.

Court came near the end of our harvest. To no surprise for Tommy but a major disappointment to Michael and I, the courtroom was once again over-booked; and we were sent home after paying Tommy another twenty-five hundred dollars. Our new trial date was set for February 2000. By this time, we could hardly remember being busted. We still were unsure of who had turned us in and didn't spend much time worrying about court anymore. At this point, we just wanted to get it over with.

The harvest of 1999 bored me so much. I filled my journal only with thoughts of things that interested me—pot growing no longer made the grade. Pages of words scribbled so badly that even I couldn't decipher them were indicators of my true feelings. I was far more interested in perfecting my technique for the perfect loaf of bread than making wads of money from pot plants. Daisy was brilliant and beautiful, an energetic creature full of humor and wonder. The latest strain of pot to grow and fail was merely a draining waste of energy.

But we did harvest pot that year, and I do remember the highlights. The latest experiment had been a strange plant that could only be grown from seed. With no mother to provide consistent clones, the plants were varied and disappointing. Some were tall and lean, some were bushy and fat and many were hermaphrodites full of pollen-filled balls that threatened the entire crop.

And it rained a lot in September, something this new strain hated. Michael couldn't afford the dripper system and bags full of nutrients specifically designed for the strain and the plants suffered further. They fluffed up and filled with mold, producing very little pot.

Grizzly was full of cold-shocked plants that desperately needed sun to finish. One cold night had sent everything backwards, and it would take weeks for the plants to recover. Lower String had only a few plants, but we managed a decent harvest out of them. A deer had eaten every single plant we put there early in the year, and we ran out of replacements. Most of the crop consisted of bottoms that had rejuvenated, and we felt lucky to have any pot at all.

James came back for what would be his last year and brought along his new girlfriend, Myana. Julie returned, out-clipping everyone by a landslide, now Michael's number-one employee. Billy-Bob's wife Marsha joined the crew, bringing stability and reason to a group of chronic drinkers and dope smokers.

One of Julie's eyes closed almost completely when she was really stoned; and she babbled incessantly, the babble of a girl who was in love with a man who didn't own a toothbrush. Her scissors flew, though, and she loved to clip pot.

James was in less than perfect form, tired and fat after a year off spent traveling and drinking with the new girlfriend. The crew got

171

along well and clipped forty-three pounds in two weeks. The only true disaster to happen that fall was the cutting down of Michael's best mother plants.

James was in charge of hiking to the patches each day and bringing a fresh load of pot to clip. There is nothing worse than trying to clip wilted pot—it takes twice as long and the end result is always a mess with more pot stuck to the scissors and fingers of the clipper than in the bag. So, James would hike around every morning enjoying the exercise while keeping the supply of marijuana fresh and crisp.

Michael marked eight plants that were *not* to be clipped, the best five destined to be next year's precious mothers. The markers were obvious—tall green stakes in the ground beside each plant with a nametag to identify the strain.

Michael actually fell to his knees in shock when he saw the stubs of what had been his mothers.

"Oh, God. This can't be, this can't be happening. What have they done?" he cried softly, kneeling in the wet brush under the remains of a great mother. "I'm finished. I give up." He remained on the ground, tears streaming down his face mixed with dirt from his hands and soft, floating drops of rain. He stared at the sky, unmoving, until his breathing returned to normal and the last heaving sob left his body. How could he ever face James?

There were other moms at home and cuttings of experimental strains started, but no Z-1 mothers. This was our best strain. How could such a thing happen? No more Z-1 mothers, the strain that came off every year in rain or shine or mold or frost.

Never had Michael been so depressed, defeated. An unfinished house, criminal charges against him and his wife, a huge lawyer's bill, mortgages with an obscene interest rate, no savings, no pot buyer, very little self-esteem and, now, no Z-1 mothers. He felt like killing himself so Daisy and I could collect his life insurance and start again. There was nowhere to go but up from a low so painfully all-encompassing.

* * *

Every year since 1994 we had planned a staff party, but one had never materialized. This was largely due to the fact Michael and I were so sick of marijuana by the time it was finally harvested that we wanted nothing more to do with it. We were sick of wage advances, complaining employees, pot deals going sour, people trying to borrow money and the constant worry over drying and selling the pot.

We had completely lost our buyer by 1996 and had been scrambling every fall since. Someone always came through with cash, but it often took driving to another province or meeting unsavory people in some dark, stinky hotel room; and the price had continued to drop.

This year, we had promised to have a party; and we intended to keep the promise—the crew had earned a big night out.

The evening began with everyone meeting at a hotel and checking into his or her respective room in a nearby city. Michael, Tony and I went shopping to get each crewmember a gift, and then we met at a restaurant recommended by Billy-Bob.

The booze started to flow; I stupidly challenged James to a drinking contest. I thought because I was Irish I'd have a fighting chance of taking on an old guy with a bloated liver. I was never more wrong about anything. James drank me into a near-coma by midnight; and I only pulled myself out of a deep, fuzzy hole with the aid of drugs and coffee. I don't know what I took, but it was something Adam had given us earlier in the year. Tony took it, too, unwilling to face the night in his usual shy silence. When we reached a strip club, also recommended by Billy-Bob, I lay down on two chairs I'd pulled together and yelled, "Bring on the whores!"

Tim thought this was fitting and joined me in my chorus, his freshly scraped teeth bared in anticipation. Billy-Bob was in awe of all the "sets" in the room, his favorite part of the female form.

"Jesus Christ, Mikey! Look at the set on that one. Fuck, I'll bet she could choke a bastard to death with them things."

Close to being asked to leave, we retreated to a casino for a change of scenery. Marsha got a bucket of change and played the slot machines. James gambled away most of his money at the blackjack table while Myana looked on with encouragement. Michael and Billy cruised around the room playing the odd game and hanging out with Marsha.

Tim was kicked out immediately for smoking pot on the sidewalk in front of the casino; Julie slunk out behind him, her right eye almost completely shut. Tony and I left after only minutes, offended by the bright, sterile room filled with machines making *Plink! Plunk! Ring! Ring!* noises. In my current state, I needed a soft, quiet place devoid of drunken people and blaring slot machines.

For lack of anyplace better, Tony and I ended up in a large country-and-western bar. The room was filled with line-dancing cowboys and cowgirls in duded up satin shirts. Oh, God, how was I going to make it through the night? Soon, our drunken comrades from the casino found us, and I was blessed with a second wind. The party continued minus only Tim and Julie; we danced and hooted and drank like there was no tomorrow.

A tall, thin girl with cropped red hair and an incredible smile approached me with a question. I said something that made her laugh, and she told me I was the nicest person she had met in the last six months. I asked her to join us, and she took one look at Tony and fell in love.

It couldn't have been more perfect if I had planned it myself. By the end of the night, Tony and his new friend Faith had checked into a motel room. Tony was finally de-flowered by a beautiful, confident, intelligent girl who found him irresistible—mission accomplished at last!

The disheveled, hung-over and emotional group parted ways in the morning, everyone grateful for the end of the season. Michael was actually calm and content as he and James embraced tightly. I felt tears welling up in my throat as my aching eyes scanned over the group.

I hugged Michael as hard as I could, sensing the possibility of the return of my former husband. Somewhere in the flurry of activity, amidst the hurdles and the triumphs, his ego had been restored. Referred to by many as a force of nature, he was proving himself as a warrior. Nothing would consume him and break his spirit as the last two years of his life had. Michael was back.

The party signified the official end of our outdoor year. Jacob and Kevin still had plants out at Lost World—tall, pale-green and budless. In November, they cut everything down and attempted to make oil. This was also an utter failure. The two men had lost fifteen thousand dollars and wasted six months growing an indoor strain of pot outdoors. I would not have a summer job next year.

Kevin would never grow outdoors again, and Jacob would start to listen to the advice of long-time growers. Michael continued to plod away at indoor, our new house still an incredible money-eating machine with an insatiable appetite. As the millennium approached, we had no interest in anything other than keeping our farm.

YEAR NINE, 2000

Tempting Fate

"The police know about the house? The police!" I screamed at Michael. "You promised me that nothing could happen this time, you said we were safe. Jesus, Michael! What are we going to do?"

We had rented another grow house in a small village close to home. Once again, the outdoor harvest and falling pot prices had been unable to support us and allow us to finish the house. We were not ready to give up yet. Michael had tried to cover all the bases this time, determined to never face police charges again.

He hired a junkie acquaintance of his to put the power bill in his name; and Ronnie's truck, which Michael had just inherited, was parked in front of the house. We tried to service the place only when it was dark, sure we couldn't get caught this time—the house belonged to a dead guy and a heroin addict was in charge of the utilities.

Two months into the project, a realtor friend sent us a message that a snoopy old lady living next to the unoccupied house had complained to the police. According to the realtor, the police had the house slated for surveillance.

* * *

FEBRUARY 2—*It's taken me a while to see my life clearly; I think I can finally identify the problem.*

176

> *Michael and I have a bad habit, and the habit is growing pot. The whole process has become deeply ingrained in every aspect of our life, and we keep doing it without even being conscious of our actions. Breaking this habit—like breaking any other—is going to take serious effort and commitment. We may not even succeed right away and must allow ample time for the transition.*

Entire industries have been built around deprogramming the smoker, the drinker, the overeater. Nowhere is there a club for pot growers who want to stop but can't. So completely immersed were we in the world we had created, Michael and I realized we had both forgotten how to do anything but grow dope. My nursing skills had lapsed, his abilities to deal with the public had all but disappeared and the debt load we had acquired was astronomical. Huge gaps in our resumes would leave prospective employers wondering what we had been doing for the past ten years.

I thought about the fact that only two of my close friends were not from the Pot World. The reality of the "straight world" was something foreign and frightening to both of us.

But, for the first time in nearly a decade, we were united. Michael agreed our sojourn into the marijuana cultivation business had run its course. And the interesting thing about our decision was that quitting would have nothing to do with the fact growing marijuana was illegal—the law *is* ignored because of its utter absurdity. Quitting was a necessity born of struggle, failure and disaster.

* * *

The neighbor hadn't complained about the usual things that neighbors bicker about; there were no loud parties, no barking dog, no messy yard. But she had read an article in the *Vancouver Sun* telling you how to do your own detective work, spy on your neighbors and turn them in to the police for growing pot when you had gathered enough circumstantial evidence.

We were never there, the curtains were always closed and the windows she had managed to crawl up to and peer through revealed a lack of furniture. This was cause to repeatedly call the rental agency—and, eventually, the police—and complain.

"We're going to tear the house down and get everything the hell out of there. That's what we're going to do. Fuck, it's like we just can't win, Princess. I'm so sorry."

As we made the drive to the abandoned house, Michael and I faced the fact we were finished. My friend Dave, who had delivered the message from the realtor, helped Michael and I tear down the grow room and clean the house. In three hours, Dave and Michael had all the wet dirt and newly planted clones in garbage bags in the back of Ronnie's truck. Michael dismantled his equipment while Dave and I cleaned and painted. As we painted the bedroom nearest the front door and small lawn, we spotted the snoopy neighbor.

Dave yelled in disgust, immediately knowing whom the woman was and hating her for all the trouble she had caused us. Michael stormed out the front door and confronted her where she was hiding behind a hedge, crouched down, peering at the house from her secret vantage point.

"Can I help you with something?" he yelled into the bush.

"Uh, um, I was just checking for fires," the woman stammered breathlessly, rising to her feet and coming out into the open. "If I don't keep these bushes clear there could be a fire."

"A fire, in February, with three feet of snow on the ground? I don't think so. Why don't you quit staring at us and just go on home."

He came back into the house, shaking his head in disgust. Inside the freshly painted bedroom, I was fuming. I had never wanted to hit anyone so badly as I did the snoopy, meddling woman.

Dave and I had watched out the window as Michael talked to the nervous spy. How ridiculous she looked, hiding behind a shrub in brightly colored clothing, too afraid to stand up and face us. It was lucky for her we were gentle, passive types. Blatantly turning people in to the police and causing them grief and embarrassment was a dangerous game to play. If we had been hardened criminals, that lady could have been beaten or robbed or God knows what.

She never knew we knew she had turned us in, and we were gone by the next day. By the time the police got to the house it was clean and empty.

We once again discussed leaving our farm behind and letting it be repossessed so we could start over. Michael was adamant about trying to hang on for one more year, so we agreed to do all we could to save our home. There was to be no extra grow house ever again. Any pot we grew would be grown outside, far away from home.

* * *

Tommy came for a sleepover the night before court, and we briefly discussed our case—this had become standard procedure, as we lived seventy miles apart. I wasn't even nervous as the big day loomed in my near future. I expected it to be an utter waste of time and just another frustrating postponement. The judge was sympathetic to our dragged-out case; and, although he did postpone, he told us we did not have to appear in court again. He heard evidence from our lawyer while the crown was given time to ready their case and submit it in writing. A date in May was set for him to hand down his decision.

We did appear with Tommy on the day that would finally be our day in court. It took sixteen thousand five hundred dollars, four court appearances and fourteen months for us to be cleared of all charges. The evidence to obtain a search warrant given by the police was completely inadequate. All the lies and confusing details and utter bullshit really did mean nothing in a court of law. The only thing the police had ever had on us was the word of their "unknown informant" of "unproven reliability."

The Canadian Charter of Rights and Freedoms protects its citizens well. All the power bills, hydroponics stores under surveillance and heat-seeking helicopters in the world don't give the police a right to kick in your door and rip your house apart—even if it is full of marijuana. The evidence presented to a judge or justice of the peace has to be very substantial—an informant usually needs to have seen pot and be willing to testify to it to get a conviction. Circumstantial evidence is useless, and many cases like ours do not result in a conviction for the police.

I involuntarily hugged a beaming Tommy and thanked him profusely. Michael and I were no longer criminals, just average Canadian citizens who happened to grow a little pot and get away with it.

* * *

With all the fear and paranoia far behind us, we planned a big outdoor year for our last. Grizzly would hold four to five hundred, Michael's acreage four hundred, Lower String one hundred and fifty and a new Billy-Bob area eighty. For this, we would need over a thousand clones.

I started planting seeds in trays of potting soil in March. By April, I had planted over four thousand. Michael cloned from some new mothers he had acquired from a friend; the plants were supposed to be very similar to the precious mothers lost to James's drunken hands at the end of our last season. Our kitchen table held hundreds of seedlings, as did the spare bedroom and library. We set up our greenhouse to accommodate the large number of clones and crossed our fingers.

Many of our pot-growing friends noticed my success with the seeds, and I was hired to make and transplant clones and seedlings. I was paid one dollar per clone and could cut and plant around four hundred clones a day. While I was working for one friend, another young, successful grower stopped by and hired me on the spot. I finished the first job and moved on to the next. I transplanted fifteen hundred clones for a generous hourly wage, Michael and I ecstatic with my earnings. All the money went directly to our mortgage and helped buy extra supplies for our outdoor crop.

As luck would have it, the spring was unusually cold, and many anxious growers lost their entire crops before June. Word of our burgeoning greenhouse got around, and we sold hundreds of clones and sexed female seedlings. This brought in thousands of dollars, and we felt positive about our future for the first time in years.

Determined to never be broke again, we stashed money and cut corners. I used recycled dirt for every hole and bag we had. For two years, I had collected dirt from all of my friends who grew indoors in soil. I would drive from house to house with a trailer or truck and load up the used dirt; I then brought it home and hid it in a pile to be leached by rain and snow. After sifting through the huge mound, I added lime and removed any unwanted traces of growing media or stalks. Michael bought me a soil-test kit to ensure the dirt was good, and from there we hauled it to the different areas.

Michael traded clones for the use of a backhoe for one day. He had huge, deep holes dug and a new waterline trench. We filled the holes with rock wool from the big room the police had taken. We were ready to plant the property ahead of schedule and had money for a helper, so Michael began his annual search. The search led him to an old friend's husband who was out of work and itching for physical activity. His name was Gino.

Gino was forty-three and had emigrated from Yugoslavia. He was six-feet-three and weighed two hundred and fifty pounds. This guy made Cousin Jimmy look like a fairy princess. Of course, Gino liked to drink—but only in spurts. He could go months without a drink and then binge for a few days until he ran out of money. His wife and two children kept a close eye on him and generally things were okay. Michael hired Gino for spring start-up, and both men were enthusiastic about the year ahead.

I accompanied them on their first day. We prepared Lower String for the dripper system and used new bales of dirt and ten-gallon bags. Gino's job was to walk almost half a mile downhill with a tightly wrapped seventy-pound bale of dirt on his back and then up the hill empty to get another bale. The overgrown bush was hard to navigate, brambles, branches and sticks slapping us in the face with every step. I made about five trips and spent the remainder of the day filling bags with dirt and nutrients. Gino made twenty-five trips. He never ate lunch or took a break until it was time to go home. And this was the most out-of-shape he had ever been. Had we finally found the perfect employee after all these years?

Filthy and exhausted, I drove home alone ahead of the men to pick Daisy up and make a late dinner. That was the last time I would

181

go to work in the bush—other than on our private land. Now thirty-five, I just couldn't keep up the demanding pace. I felt I would be far more useful at home looking after Daisy and washing work clothes and cooking and baking than trying to prove myself in the bush. My wonderful husband agreed; he had never wanted me to work, anyway, but couldn't stop me from insisting on coming.

* * *

JUNE 4—*The sun was that perfect temperature that warms your skin but never becomes uncomfortable or hot, and a breeze sifted through the new leaves on the birch trees, rattling them hypnotically. The chorus of birds, as they called to each other, filled the cool air above my head. It's days like today that I will miss; the peace I feel when I'm working on the acreage Michael and I share with marijuana. I am so grateful for the life I have. When I see a photograph or a news clip of a magnificent city, all I see is chaos and concrete. I wonder how they all do it, how they live like that crammed on top of each other fighting for space and privacy. I feel sick if I think about living without a garden or a field full of grass to run in. The last nine years of my life haven't been without happiness and fulfillment.*

My job was easy and enjoyable—no physical labor involved. Fill a bag with the used dirt we had hauled in and then add bat guano, slow-release fertilizer, rock dust and bone meal. With a facemask and rubber gloves on, I'd stir and fluff the contents of one bag before starting on the next. I worked alone as Michael hauled supplies to the various patches with his quad.

After several hours, I heard the motor of the little bike over the tranquil sounds of the forest. I stood up and watched for Michael to crest the hill I was working on, cramped from hours of squatting and dying for an excuse to have a break.

As I stood up, a bolt of yellow shot across the road in front of me. My brain slowed to focus on the immediate situation. That couldn't have been a cougar that had just darted out across the road.

I had finally started carrying bear mace everywhere I went; my can lay on a bag of dirt inches away from me. I grabbed it and pulled the safety off, scanning the thick trees for signs of movement. My legs were shaking; why wasn't Michael here yet?

I knew nothing about cougars except that they were powerful and secretive—I hoped to never encounter one in the bush. I was honored to have glimpsed the magnificent cat but felt as though I were on the verge of vomiting. The cougar had probably been watching me from its spot beneath the branches of a tall fir tree, a creepy, eerie thought. The sound of the motor approaching and my standing up must have startled the animal and caused it to run.

Michael finally appeared. Frozen to the ground with my heart pounding in loud thumps and my right hand glued to the can of bear mace, I told him what had just happened.

We walked, tightly holding hands, to look for tracks in the soft dirt under the tree. We found nothing—it was as if I had imagined the whole thing. Believing me, and certain it had been a cougar, Michael promised to never leave me alone again, not even for a minute.

For the last year, he had found rabbit paws, fur and entrails on the ground all over his property. An avid watcher and lover of birds, he had also noticed the grouse population had slowly diminished. Our area was known for its cougar population; it was actually remarkable that neither of us had ever encountered one before. I would never feel the same at the acreage where we had always gardened, hiked and picnicked without any sort of protection.

"I'm glad it's our last year, Mike. I'm too old for this shit." I laughed. "He sure was magnificent, though. His tail must have been three feet long. Think of all the people who live their whole life and never get to see something like that. I only wish you could have been here with me."

I hopped onto the back of the quad and waited for him.

* * *

Gino came back to continue preparing the wild grow areas with Michael. His first day back was spent close to home, and the men returned for a late dinner. The next week they would be camped across the lake at Grizzly and other patches far from home. Michael packed the truck with camping gear and supplies while Gino snuck down to the store for beer.

At first, it was hard to tell when he was drunk because Gino had a strange way of speaking. He talked in riddles and short, disjointed sentences, which always left me nodding and pretending to understand him when really I wouldn't have a clue what he was talking about. When his brain reached a certain point with alcohol, he became unbearable and completely impossible to understand.

"Yeah. Do you know what I'd really like? Tits. Just an open blouse and some tits. Falling out into the, yeah. You know? Is that asking a lot? God, just to see some tits." This was our new employee at the dinner table his second day on the job.

After all the alcoholics we had hired, I didn't know if I could take another one. Michael defended his new ox-like employee and said, "It's not like he's drunk all the time, Princess, and it's only once. Let's just let it go; give the guy a break."

"It better be just this once, Michael. I can't take another alcoholic. What are we going to do if he does this all the time? I don't *want* to talk about tits at the dinner table, even it's only once in a while."

"Don't worry, hon. If you knew how bad he had it at home, you'd understand. He's just letting off a little steam. Mary hasn't had sex with him in over a year, you know. Can you believe that? What a bitch."

"Actually, I can see why. Maybe he does this all the time, and she's totally repulsed by him. Anyway, we'll let it go for today; but I sure hope it's not some kind of pattern."

I finished washing the dishes and called Daisy in for bed. By now, Gino was wandering around the yard talking to the llamas, chickens and cats—anything that would listen. Beer cans were hidden in trees and on fence posts, in flowerpots, in the hayfield.

Dad stopped by to visit after dinner and was flabbergasted by the questions and senselessness of Gino's conversation.

"Mary-Ann, what the fuck is that guy talking about? I haven't understood a word he's saying." Dad giggled as he gestured towards Gino, who by now was sitting near a huge mound of llama manure gazing up at the sky.

The pointless riddles that couldn't be answered had us all stumped and laughing. I couldn't wait for the long camping trip and hoped for Michael's sake Gino wasn't drunk and unbearable.

A few days later, Michael called from his parent's cabin. Grizzly was prepped and ready to plant, and Gino and he were getting along great. There had been no booze on the trip to Grizzly, but the cabin was a five-minute walk to a liquor outlet. Even better, Michael's parents had a bar at their cabin; and it took Gino only minutes to locate it. While Michael showered, Gino started drinking.

I got another call from Michael early the next morning. He was whispering, and I could tell he was pissed off; but I had trouble understanding him. He was trying to tell me that Gino had peed on the counter of his mother's kitchen.

I sat up stiffly in bed, rubbing the sleep out of my eyes and shrieked, "What? He pissed on your mother's counter? Jesus, you better fire him! Tell me you're going to fire him. Why the fuck would he piss on the counter? In the kitchen? Oh, God, Michael. What a disaster! What are you going to do? Where did he get the booze?"

I bombarded Michael with questions—the image of Gino emptying his bladder onto the counter where Daisy and I shelled peas and ate watermelon was horrifying. He explained that, during the course of the evening, just like Goldilocks, Gino had slept in every bed in the cabin. He'd pass out in a bed, wake up, go to the bathroom or to the kitchen for a snack, and then wander into a different room and fall asleep.

By morning he was disoriented and still partly drunk, and he ended up upstairs and thought he was in the bathroom. He pointed himself in the direction of the toilet, which was an entire floor beneath him, took aim and fired. He happened to fire directly into the little kitchen, the splattering sound waking Michael as the droplets hit the counter and drizzled down the cupboards onto the floor. When Michael ran into the kitchen, all he saw was a stream of urine hitting his mother's dishes and soaking the food on the counter. He yelled at Gino to wake him, and the torrent subsided.

I never fully grasped why this was okay, but Michael had enormous patience and empathy for drunks. Gino's employment continued. The two men had a heart-to-heart, and Gino agreed to be on a two-drink limit. Michael's tolerance astounded me; it was as if he were immune to the glaring faults of his employees.

A few days later, Willy came to visit; and we headed to the cabin to meet Michael after work. Daisy, Willy and I cooked dinner and played Yahtzee, too hot to go outside and face the setting sun. Drained, aching and late, the two weary men finally rolled in. Michael was thrilled with the surprise visit and dinner, but he was upset about the loss of a patch.

Always eager to experiment, Michael had delegated his smallest patch for a test plot. It would be all organic, and he would apply kelp, with a sprayer, once a week. After the first application, every single plant had withered and died.

It took careful thought and study to determine the cause of death. The leaves were crispy and discolored, and the entire length of each plant looked as if a giant syringe had been inserted into the stalk, sucking the very life from the healthy young plants. The leaves were splattered with a pattern of whitish spots, leading Michael to believe that something applied with a sprayer had done the damage.

But he had sprayed nothing but kelp. One of Michael's new two-hundred-pound-per-year idols had recommended it. An organic plant derivative itself, how could sea kelp do such a thing? Was the mixture too strong? Was the friend that told him to use it mistaken or out to sabotage him? Thoughts bombarded Michael's brain like bullets, and he squeezed his head with dirt- and blood-caked hands.

A few plants had been packed home as samples; and we dragged them into the bathtub, hoping to revive them by leaching the mystery substance out. After having gallons of cold water dumped on them, the plants looked exactly the same—dead. And then it hit us...

Tordon.

Tordon is a broad-leaf herbicide so deadly that it must be purchased and applied by someone with a license. We had hired someone to spray our farm for weeds the previous year, and he had been too busy to return. Desperate, we had acquired some of the chemical through a farmer and mixed it and sprayed it ourselves. Michael had not been thorough enough when he cleaned the sprayer and applicator nozzle before applying the latest necessary new thing to his crop.

The minute amount of the deadly herbicide had been enough to wipe out the entire patch. We were also told by Billy-Bob not to use the area again for at least one year because the ground would be saturated with the chemical. I hated Michael for experimenting *again* and didn't know why he couldn't just leave everything alone.

As if that wasn't bad enough, Gino had snuck to the store while Willy and Michael and I pondered the fate of the plants in the bathtub. He returned almost an hour later, well on his way to being drunk and talking nonsense.

"Hey, yeah. So, Willy, let's talk about Willy. Want an apple?"

Willy had just met Gino for the first time and had no idea how to respond.

"Hey, I know you guys are doing coke in there. I know, man."

To this I said, sternly, "Gino, I have no idea what you're talking about. I can assure you that Daisy and I were not snorting cocaine. She's six. And I hate cocaine. We were playing Yahtzee."

Then, Gino started telling me how beautiful I was and how lucky Michael was to have me, and I took this as my cue to leave. I was scared he would soon be telling us how he just wanted to see some tits falling out of a blouse, and I wanted no part of it. Daisy and I packed up the car, and Willy stayed behind with the men. For this, Michael was grateful.

Gino's drinking became a source of amusement and heartache all at the same time. It was too late to fire him, and he was an amazing worker in the bush. No one worked like Gino. He never complained, and he loved being out in the wilderness. He could easily do the work of two men in a day, so Michael vowed to get through the spring and quietly phase him out.

Gino loved the work so much he had offered to go out with Michael all year for nothing. He wanted to learn how to grow pot and to get away from his suffocating family. This never happened.

On a binge at the cabin one night Gino tried to walk to the nearest town for cocaine. Willy and Michael had assured him the flickering lights he saw in the distance were reachable on foot; the nearest town was seventy miles away. When it became obvious that the lights were beyond his grasp after hours of walking, he called his wife from a pay phone; and she drove out and picked him up. That was Gino's last shift.

Michael worked alone for the rest of the year, and he worked hard. I enjoyed a relaxed summer just being a mother. Daisy was now six and able to swim, and she enjoyed nothing more than water. I worked early in the morning before the heat became unbearable, and most afternoons Daisy and I swam and collected rocks at a nearby beach. We picked cherries and strawberries together, and Daisy started her own little garden, squealing in delight as her pumpkins took shape and flowers burst open in neat little rows.

* * *

> JULY 20—*Lisa's Stag; what a riot! Fifteen girls showed up for a three-day weekend full of singing, dancing, eating and drinking. The weather was perfect and Michael's mother managed to stay away the whole time, trusting me to return the cabin to its original condition. I met some wonderful girls—my favorite a girl named Mikayla who works with Lisa.*

On the second day, we all dressed up and ventured out to a summer restaurant and bar on the lake. Within ten minutes, half the girls in our party were cut off and asked to leave. Our designated drivers left the more sober of us behind and rescued the trouble-causers. Those of us who remained gathered at one large table, and soon men in the bar were trying to join us.

This was forbidden, it being a girls-only stag weekend. I quickly told the one man at our table that, due to the fact he had a penis, he had to leave. It was then I was informed he was a cop—a drug squad cop, in fact. That, I told him, was definitely reason enough for him to find another table, but it was too late. His partner was also on his way over, and they were apparently good customers of most of the girls at the party, who worked at a beautiful, uptown neighborhood pub that was frequented by the police officers who worked nearby. The partner just happened to be the undercover cop who helped arrest me and had probably gone through my underwear drawers.

I spent the remainder of the afternoon forced to make small talk with Officer Longhair. He was drunk and sleazy, hustling all the gorgeous young girls while his wife of thirteen years remained at home with their children. As the sun went down, we were offered a ride back to Michael's family cabin on the Narcboat, as the girls called it. I had to accept and join the rest of the group, cringing as Officer Longhair stared at my breasts as I leaned into the boat.

No longer in the mood for a party, I wanted only to be with my family; two days of sun and partying had tired me out, anyway. Michael and Daisy hurried to the cabin to rescue me. He was shocked to hear of our chance meeting with the boating drug cops, but reminded me we did live on a very popular lake. And it hadn't actually been that awful—I pretended I hadn't seen a pot plant in two years, and the cop pretended he'd never arrested me.

With Gino gone and the year half-over, Michael and I finally spent time together. Seeing light at the end of the tunnel of debt, the old Michael was totally back. Jokes and silliness prevailed; we had no partner to worry about and things in the Pot World were looking good. Michael did plan on being his own guard this fall, so we tried to squeeze in lots of family time before Daisy went back to school and her dad went to the bush.

Willy came to visit for a weekend and ended up staying over a month. He went to work with Michael for beer and cigarettes, more mature and helpful than he'd ever been. We also spent a lot of time with our friend Dave. He was in a dysfunctional relationship and really drinking and dabbling in drugs. Every time Carrie hit him in the

189

head with a frying pan he ended up wandering along the road half-naked with a bottle of vodka in his hand or driving his truck through a fence.

Dave had lost his driver's license, and Michael or I drove him to his patches in exchange for work. Surrounded by young, able-bodied men, Michael had company and help for the remainder of the season.

The sun was overcome by rain and cool weather by September. I had taken a professional clipping job for fifty dollars an hour and was content to work indoors. Five days a week, I drove to a hidden community sprawled over a dry hillside. Draft dodgers fleeing the Vietnam War in the late 1960s had settled the area. Everybody smoked and grew pot. It had been a way of life passed down through the generations, father and mother taught daughter and son; grandparents were dope-smoking, respected elders with bags of money buried in their yards. This thriving alcove of hippies succeeded because everything was kept in the family.

Slightly inbred, the families swapped wives and husbands and girlfriends. Everyone was somehow related to someone from one of the founding families. There were no informants or finks; the common goal was the good of the community.

Carmella had lived in a tepee on the hill when she first arrived in the area and had introduced me to several of her friends. After seven years of potlucks and dances and solstice parties, I was trusted enough to be hired. I was also a pot grower who was dedicated to the craft and of Irish descent. This was truly the greatest job I had ever had.

After years of failure and disaster, our luck seemed to finally be changing. All of Michael's plants were surpassing his humble estimates, I was making five hundred dollars a day and the smallest successes seemed like the moon to us.

Dave had inherited a patch of three hundred from a very wealthy grower. The patch had been discovered shortly after it was planted, so the owner offered it to his laborers—Dave and a buddy named Simon. The two men accepted the offer but no one had seen the patch since May. Dave, in need of a driver and vehicle, offered us a third for transporting the plants to a clip house. Simon was busy clipping for someone else and would do almost nothing for his third, but how could we refuse? Michael and I made several trips to the abandoned patch that we called Cowboy.

Cows had gone through the patch all year long, leaving overturned bags and plants smeared with cow shit. The watering system had never been checked, and many plants had dried up and died. No nutrients had been added to the soil since May, and the plants were in rough shape; but the patch was still intact.

When Dave first told me about it, I was immediately negative and said, "There's no way a patch that size will still be there. If someone drove through it on a quad and let their cows loose in it, they will definitely have ripped off the patch. Nothing this good could possibly happen to a bunch of losers like us, Dave. There's got to be a catch."

I was never more wrong. We made three trips into Cowboy and harvested twenty-three pounds. The buds were small and cold-shocked, but we spent hours painstakingly grooming the pot to make it acceptable. On the last trip in, Michael went with Dave and Simon while I worked for the hippies.

The police had finally found the patch. They cut the remaining branches down, slashed the waterline, threw the expensive components into the bush, slashed every bag to bits and pulled the dripper system apart. But Dave had told Michael a story about how a friend of his had just lost a patch to the police and found all of his pot thrown in a heap in the bush nearby. Michael vowed to find the missing branches.

"Just one leaf is all we need, guys. I'm going to take a look around and see if I can't find where they dumped it." Michael stalked off into the bush like a bloodhound, sniffing, searching, circling the area.

Cowboy was on a plateau hidden deep in the bush, a long way from a road and surrounded by deep ravines. Having a hunch that the RCMP weren't athletic enough to haul all the pot out, a determined Michael found one wilted branch, which led him to a large bundle containing the rest of the pot. The cold September nights in the shaded ravine had protected it, and it was as fresh as if we had just cut it down.

The last load was hauled to the clip house, and once again straw was spun into gold. Michael and I planned to return to Cowboy, convinced we could find the timers and salvage other equipment. We also wanted to clean up the field, which the police had left littered with plastic.

* * *

On September 9th, a day off from my clipping job, Mikayla came to visit. She loved to smoke pot and had recently quit her job, leaving her broke, bored and depressed. Interested in learning how to clip pot and make some extra money, she packed up her little car and made the journey to our pot-growing mecca.

"Hi, honey," Mikayla yelled as she swung her car into the driveway.

I was sitting on the front porch having tea with Daisy and got up lazily to greet my new friend. "Hey, sweetie, how are you doing? You're early."

"Yeah, baby. I'm ready to work! Show me how it's done, Mary-Ann. I'm here to work the scissors."

We had a light snack, called Michael in to take Daisy to a friend's house and snuck into the hidden room to practice clipping. We had the remains of a few plants in bud, and I gave my pupil a quick run-through of the job.

I looked over at Mikayla, her shiny blond hair filled with sticky green clippings and her tongue gently pressed between her teeth. Her scissors carefully moved around each little bud with love and attention to detail. She was an apt pupil, and I deemed her ready to take the plunge into professional clipping.

I was fighting flu, and we had to drive for over an hour to Michael's secluded cabin where the final buckets of pot from Cowboy awaited us. Mikayla offered to drive, and I gratefully took her up on the offer, my energy level deteriorating. We loaded her tiny car with food, clothing and supplies and headed across the lake. After only a few hours, I had to pack it in.

I was shivering and sweating, my nose pouring that liquid snot that always signifies the beginning of something awful. Stupidly, I had put the wet, freshly clipped pot into a plastic grocery-store bag and thrown it into the car. The pot was starting to mold and there was nowhere to dry it in the shack we were using, so I thought I'd take it home.

Neither Mikayla nor I was worried about it a bit. I was so sick I didn't care about anything but getting home for a hot bath. Mikayla wasn't a paranoid person and felt safe in the sparsely populated wilderness community. Only minutes from the shack, the little car chugged down a steep hill into a police roadblock. I couldn't believe I had been stupid enough, or unlucky enough, to be arrested a second time.

* * *

I believe in fate. It was always my fate to be punished to the full extent of the law for growing pot. This was not Michael's fate, though, and I find that fascinating. Sherry and Tony always tell me I am the most indiscreet person they know. It's true. I actually can't believe it took so long for me to be caught again.

I continued to clip pot for money and watched Michael pull off his best year in a long time. Tommy was acting as counsel for both Mikayla and me. Five days after our arrest, the police had decided to bring charges against Mikayla as well as me. Our first court appearance on September 27th resulted in nothing more than a subsequent trial date for December. I waited patiently and assured Mikayla she had nothing to worry about.

Partway through October, the outdoor year was finished. We had fifty-two pounds of pot, and I had earned eight thousand dollars. Michael paid off every small loan we had, and we zero-balanced our credit cards before cutting them all in half. It was tempting to change our minds about the pact we had made; but my arrest and Michael's aging, aching body overshadowed the modest success of the year.

Year Ten, 2001

The End of an Era

Quitting the Pot World meant giving up our farm. Losing the home we had worked so hard to keep was like losing the air from my lungs. I couldn't breathe.

The worst part was finding a home for the llamas. I couldn't bear the thought of not seeing them every morning and being nuzzled over the fence by Felix. Normally cold and steely, I bawled like a baby over the loss of my animal friends as I accepted the fact we were leaving. We had enough money to start over, but nowhere near enough to pay off our home. Our mortgage broker took over our little dream world, and we slowly began to pack our belongings.

Three days before Christmas 2000, I pled guilty to possession of marijuana. I had provided Tommy with a picture of a huge pot plant that I claimed was the one responsible for my new drug charges. I had learned to lie almost as well as my husband and believed I couldn't be in too much trouble for growing just one plant.

The judge totally believed my confession, or maybe he didn't think it was relevant—I grew one outdoor plant that just happened to be monstrous. The picture was passed around the little courtroom, evoking giggles and raised eyebrows from everyone who studied it. The production of a controlled substance charge was dropped, as well as the intent to traffic. For the possession of one kilogram of wet pot, estimated to weigh less than a third of that dry, I was given a two hundred-fifty-dollar fine and asked kindly if I needed time to pay it. Mikayla was cleared of all charges and given a conditional discharge.

After nine years of law-defying luck, I finally got a criminal record for possession of marijuana. Like the man who tattoos his lover's name on his forearm, the government had given me my first inerasable ink rendering of my favorite plant. I have officially paid my dues.

* * *

The only thing different about me now that I am a convicted criminal is that I cannot travel to the USA—a war-loving country fraught with racism where my dollar is worth about sixty-five cents and the war on drugs is flourishing. I think I can happily live out the rest of my life without going to the United States.

So, at the end of ten years, most of the money we made we had spent foolishly or couldn't account for at all. Daisy's bus driver and our neighbor scorned us for being drug dealers, and I am officially a criminal.

But the things we learned about greed, friendship, love and loyalty will stay with us forever. We don't desire a big, fancy house—we're happy in an old two-bedroom that's close to Michael's college. We don't need any new friends—the ones that have stuck by us through all the shit we've been in are more than enough. I don't want a new husband—the man I fell in love with is easier to see when he's not frantically trying to make a million dollars. He's right in front of me.

When people ask me if it was worth it, I say yes. When people ask me if I'd recommend it, I say no. I will continue to vote as long as there is a Marijuana Party, and I feel strongly that pot will be legalized in the next five years…and we'll never really miss the Pot World because so many of our dear friends and neighbors are firmly in its grip.

UPDATES

Adam: After breaking up with April and battling an addiction to speed, Adam worked on a fish farm on Vancouver Island for two years. He's now strong and healthy, dating the stripper of his dreams. Adam makes his living middling pot and selling ecstasy.

April: April is enrolled in college full time and has been for the past three years. She clips pot for extra money and is unbelievably good at it. We all have high hopes for April's future.

Aunty Kenny: Kenny's home and place of business burned to the ground in February 2001—I suppose his whole life will start over once the insurance check comes in. He may never have to grow another pot plant as long as he lives.

Azim: After almost a decade in Canada, Azim finally made enough money to return to Afghanistan and never came back.

Billy-Bob and Marsha Washburn: The Washburns have become very good friends. Billy still rents areas to pot growers but makes his living raising beef cattle and logging. Marsha runs four commercial greenhouses supplying bedding plants, vegetables and herbs to our community. Whenever we have time to get together with the Washburns, we do.

Bob and Liza Hudson: Bob and Liza have separated, and Liza has filed for divorce. Bob has lost thirty pounds from his terrible addiction to crack and lost his business and home. He also lost his drivers license and has been charged with fraud and assault. After his three years as a police informant, no one in the community will speak to Bob. Liza grows outdoor successfully and is seriously involved with an alcoholic satellite salesman.

Boomer: Mathew employs Boomer to clip all of his indoor pot; he does this because he is kind, not because Boomer is good at the job. I believe this to be the only steady income in Boomer's life, so how much booze and Xanax can he be doing?

Carmella: Carmella has gained another twenty or thirty pounds and had another baby. On the verge of leaving her boyfriend—again— she is bombarding anyone willing to listen with the sordid details. I worked with Carmella for one day last fall, and she was fired at the end of the shift. We haven't spoken since.

Cousin Jimmy: Last we heard, Jimmy was working in a logging camp near the B.C./Alberta border. He is heavy and drinking excessively whenever he can. Neither Michael nor I have spoken to Jimmy since 1996, and I'm still getting over it.

Dad: My father continues to support Michael and I in any way he can. His open mind provides endless topics of conversation, and he seems excited about my book. Dad hasn't grown anything in years; but he assures us that if he were a few years younger, his acreage would be loaded with marijuana.

Daisy: Now seven years old, our beautiful little girl knows nothing about what her parents have been through over the past ten years. Daisy excels in school and is incredibly happy and well-adjusted. She knows that Mommy loves to garden, and the most important things in her life are school, her parents and her home full of pets.

Damon Murdock: After several months of hard-core drug abuse that left him badly in debt, Damon applied to the government for a student loan and got one. With his student loan, he purchased a cell phone, a pager and a whole bunch of heroin and cocaine. He prances around the bars and restaurants of his hometown, always available for business.

Dave: I honestly worry about Dave as I write his update. After a very good outdoor year, Dave bought a sailboat docked in Trinidad. He arrived to discover that he really didn't own the boat and had been set up and ripped off. Dave then stole the boat, which is technically his, and sailed it up the coast, where he hid until last month. Police stormed onto his boat and repossessed it early one morning—no one has heard from Dave since. Previous to this, we had regular contact with Dave via email. We hope for his safe return.

Doug Vandermeer: Doug passed away in January 1999. I am so happy that he was finally set free and think of him often.

Elvis: The Elvis impersonator from our temporary rented house near the hospital is still stalking the streets of small-town B.C. looking for work. Michael and I were in a Radio Shack this Christmas, and there he was. I told him I was writing a book and that he was in it. He looked at me skeptically through his yellow fishtail sunglasses and said, "I'm the best, baby."

Gino: I honestly don't think much has changed with Gino. He binges regularly and probably dreams of tits every night. Michael would never hire him again, even if he decided to grow pot in a tough area.

Henrietta: Henry has a full-time job with a small woodworking company. She continues to support her family and is always available to clip pot or do anything else that will give her extra cash. Every Christmas we go on a horse-drawn sleigh ride with Henry and her entire family, and we try to get together for a few barbeques in the summer.

Herman: Still a nocturnal drug addict, Herman collects antique toys and bizarre literature to fill his basement apartment. Herman continues to buy, sell and smoke plenty of marijuana.

Indiana Stan: Stan hastily left the province after Michael and I fired him. According to mutual acquaintances, he continues to rip people off by building houses he really doesn't know how to build. He hopes to, some day, actually learn how to build a house.

Jacob Flynn: After quitting steroids when chunks of his hair fell out and his penis all but disappeared, Jacob got right back on four months later. Engaged to be married, buff and planning a big outdoor year, Jacob has grow houses cropping up everywhere. His dad and brother are partners in several houses, and I clip for them whenever necessary. He and Michael go to Grizzly and camp for quality time together.

James Foreman: James is currently living and working in Whistler. He teaches snowboarding for the Mountain and comes highly recommended. Myana lives with James and is the only adult on the hill that wears a helmet and full body padding every time she straps on her snowboard. I think that eventually James and Myana will get married

Kevin: Kevin's twenty-five-light grow house with stolen power was raided in January 2001. Michael learned this while attending court for his assault on Rob Hudson. Kevin vanished in a fifty thousand-dollar car he had just paid cash for. As of March 2001, the grapevine tells us Tommy Dodge has been retained as Kevin's lawyer.

Michael Hokenson: Michael is now the world's oldest student, enrolled in college in the new town we live in. His love of the outdoors will keep him sane and healthy, and he is deeply loved by his wife and child. With or without the Pot World, Michael is an exciting man to be around.

Mikayla: Now one of my closest friends, Mikayla is still looking for work and spreading joy throughout the world via her incredible smile. She and her boyfriend are currently embarking on their virgin journey into the indoor Pot World. Who am I to disapprove?

Officer Fat-Ass: Shortly after the whole community learned of his wife's infidelity, Officer Fat-Ass applied for a transfer to another province.

Sherry: Growing pot in a rented house set up by Tony, Sherry only grows in dirt and resents her plants for not having bright, pretty flowers. Sherry is paying April's college tuition with the profits from her garden.

Tim and Julie: I haven't seen Tim in over a year, but I assume he's still smoking joints all day long and working only in the Pot World. Julie got a job at a gas station last spring, but I have yet to see her there. Without corrective surgery, her right eye should be completely closed by her twenty-fifth birthday.

Tommy Dodge: Still practicing law and specializing in criminal and drug law, Tommy is in fine form. We have a standing invitation to attend a nude solstice party, and I've been feeling the need to attend one soon. Hopefully, Kevin will be happy with Tommy's services as a lawyer.

Tony: Tony just got a new computer as well as a motorboat and a Skidoo. He continues to wait for Faith for his next sexual experience.

Viet: Still gangbanging in Vancouver and attending a lot of funerals, Viet remains the perfect gangster.

Willy: Willy is now twenty-five, unemployed and living in Calgary. His only job has been crop-sitting for an unorganized biker gang who were recently fined and beaten by Hell's Angels. He has a girlfriend, a dog and a Harley-Davidson.

ABOUT THE AUTHOR

Mary-Jane lives in a small town in B.C.s interior with her husband of ten years, their daughter and three old cats. She is busy working on her next book.

LOOK FOR THESE GREAT TITLES AT:
www. Zumayapublications.com

PARANORMAL FICTION

SCARY CREEK by Thomas Cater   ISBN: 1-894869-21-4
SUBTERRANEAN HEARTBEATS by Diana Kemp-Jones
ISBN: 1-59109-070-9
HOUSE OF CAPTURED FANCY by Tom Cater
ISBN: 1-894869-36-2

SCIENCE FICTION

EMBRACING THE SKULL by Martine Jardin and Diana Kemp-Jones
ISBN: 1-59109-051-2
DYSTOPIC VISIONS by Diana Kemp-Jones   ISBN: 894869-28-1
SISTERS OF THE WIND by Diana Kemp-Jones   ISBN: 1-59109-055-5
THRILLER
THE MANDYLION by Thomas Cater ISBN: 159109-069-5
TULPA by Ron Landry   ISBN: 1-894869-43-5
ROMANCE
UNORTHODOX PROPOSAL by Martine Jardin   ISBN: 1-59109-053-9
BLUEPRINT FOR REVENGE by Martine Jardin   ISBN: 1-59109-050-4
HISTORICAL FICTION
THE START OF MAGIC by Dr. Bob Rich   ISBN: 1-894869-23-0
THE MAIDEN'S SONG by Debra Tash   ISBN: 1-894869-25-7
THE PINECROFT THOROUGHBREDS by Selwyn A. Grames
ISBN: 1-59109-054-7
THE VANDALIANS by Thomas Cater   ISBN: 1-894869-47-8
HIS MAJESTY'S ENVOY by Richard Patton   ISBN: 1-894869-38-9
THE RELUCTANT COMMANDER by Richard Patton
ISBN: 1-894869-57-5
THE MOTHER'S SWORD by Dr. Bob Rich   ISBN: 1-894869-45-1
MAINSTREAM FICTION
YESTERDAY'S TEARS, TOMORROW'S PEARLS by Martine Jardin
ISBN: 1-59109-167-5
MANIPULATIONS by Shrinivas Sharangpani   ISBN: 1-894869-32-X
PARADOX OUTPATIENT by Bernie Schallehn   ISBN: 1-894869-16-8

MYSTERY

TRACETRACKS by Larry Rochelle   ISBN: 1-894869-14-1
BEN ZAKKAI'S COFFIN by Harley L. Sachs   ISBN: 1-894869-20-6
DEATH AND DEVOTION by Larry Rochelle   ISBN: 1-894869-30-3
DANCE WITH THE PONY by Larry Rochelle   ISBN: 1-894869-18-4

FANTASY

CRYSTAL DREAMS by Astrid Cooper ISBN: 1-59109-065-2
THE BLOOD CIRCLE by Ellen Anthony ISBN: 1-894869-34-6

EROTICA

SEA ORPHAN by J. Kramer ISBN: 1-59109-062-8
SCIROTICA by Cameron Hale ISBN: 1-59109-063-6
WHY SHOULD GUYS HAVE ALL THE FUN by Cindy X. Novo
ISBN: 1-894869-40-0

HORROR

THE CHRONICLES OF A MADMAN by Michael LaRocca
ISBN: 1-59109-068-7

GOTHIC

ECHOES OF ANGELS by Caitlyn McKenna ISBN:1-894869-41-9

YOUNG ADULT

FIVE DAYS TILL DAWN   ISBN: 1-894869-51-6

NON FICTION – SELF HELP

HOW TO MANAGE ANGER AND ANXIETY by Dr. Bob Rich
ISBN: 1-59109-064-4

EDUCATION

PROF RAP by Professor Larry Rochelle   ISBN: 1-89486